MIGNON FRANÇOIS

MADE
FROM *Scratch*
FINDING SUCCESS WITHOUT A RECIPE

R.H. BOYD
EST. 1896

Made from Scratch
Finding Success Without a Recipe

By Mignon François

Cover design by Jasmine Cole

Cover photography by Elijah Rodney

Cover copyright © 2023 by R.H. Boyd Publishing Corporation

R.H. Boyd Publishing Corporation
6717 Centennial Blvd.
Nashville, Tennessee 37209
rhboyd.com
Facebook/Twitter/Instagram: @RHBoyd
First Edition: May 2023

ISBN: 979-8-88365-059-3
Printed in the United States

Dedication

For my children
Alexius, Lauren, Jacques, Dillon,
Druscilla-Brittany, Xavier, and Bree

You have been my greatest teachers in life, love, forgiveness, business, and so much more. I'm proud to have been the hot mess of mistakes that God used to introduce the world to you.

We surely don't look like what we've been through—for *all things* work together for the good of them who love the Lord, and we are just one example of what that looks like.

Contents

Publisher's Note

S outhern roots are often tied to both sweetness and struggle. Life is sweeter when shared with loved ones and pursuing your purpose, which invariably brings its challenges. *Made from Scratch* is a prime example of the intersection of love and purpose. From Mignon François' impactful and inspiring story to her infectious smile, this memoir shows that nothing is impossible when strength and faith collide to make miracles happen, despite the struggles.

Cupcakes bring happiness and joy. It is hard to believe that, in this case, they originated from a season of heartache and pain. These same cupcakes have become one of the most iconic bakeries and stories of success — not only in Nashville and New Orleans, but nationwide.

When the opportunity arose to work with Mignon, it was an instant yes for me. She is an inspiration to many, and it is time the literary masses know her story. This story of how one family overcame poverty and pain to bring others happiness and joy is a distinct honor to share. R.H. Boyd takes pride in bringing stories such as these to life to help others and future generations, as we have since 1896.

Using her last five dollars to make cupcakes and building it into a ten-million-dollar enterprise is quite an impressive feat; however, the true magic of Mignon's story is not the dollar amount—it is the formidable faith and spirit of the author who makes the pages shine with wisdom and practical knowledge gleaned from very real-life experiences.

Mignon, we applaud you for your success and the love that you have bestowed on your family and community. Now is just the beginning...there is so much more joy and happiness to come...and amazing cupcakes, books, and more, too.

Dr. LaDonna Boyd
Fifth-generation President/CEO
R.H. Boyd Family of Companies

Foreword

often get requests to write book forewords. Most of the time, I have to decline these gracious invitations, and it's rarely because I don't want to do them. Truthfully, writing a foreword for an author I don't know well is challenging. It's difficult for me to endorse someone when I don't know their background, family, their history, and haven't had any genuine experiences with the individual.

But with Mignon, it's different. Knowing Mignon as I do and the history we share, the prospect of sharing my thoughts on *Made from Scratch* was a no-brainer. The time I spent in contemplative reflection preparing this foreword has been a genuine pleasure and an opportunity in which I remain humbled by and grateful for.

I went to college with Mignon's brother, where he and I were suitemates. I've known Mignon through her brother, and other New Orleans friends who have been like family, for many years.

I also know Mignon's gifts and her skill sets. I know her spirit and her energy. I know her passion, and I see the energy she brings when she walks into a room—the hope and joy she gives to others. So, when she approached me about writing the foreword to *Made from Scratch*, I agreed, knowing that her book would be a significant literary contribution to anyone on the quest for success. I'm confident her story will capture the attention of women who have dedicated their lives and made economic sacrifices to support their families, only to have their life partner walk away.

Sadly, Mignon's experience is more rule than exception. By definition, a homemaker foregos the security of a traditional nine-to-five and becomes wholly financially dependent on their spouse or partner. If that partnership doesn't work out, the homemaker must start from scratch.

I witnessed my girl Mignon start her life reset from the bottom—having the life she knew, her reality, stripped from her. Instead of giving up, giving in, and losing hope, she literally started from scratch and built an empire. I was privileged to observe how she overcame mental and emotional roadblocks to her success that would have paralyzed or destroyed others. I saw how she used her purpose and passion for God and her family to find a way out of no way.

That's why her book is so important. It contains so many gems, so many life principles, and so many strategies that are coupled with hope and inspiration. Mignon's story is a model of what a woman in her circumstance, having absolutely nothing in terms of financial resources or even business acumen, can do. Hers is also a story of what we all can do once we decide not to focus solely on what we've lost or on the trials and tribulations that may have left us feeling like we were done wrong.

When we stop focusing on what has been lost and instead start recognizing the gifts that God has given us and that only God Himself can save us, we start realizing, "Yo, I owe me." That means maturing enough to understand that, above all else, we owe it to ourselves to reframe our perspectives and accept that things happen for us, not to us or against us.

The Bible says in Proverbs 18:16 that our gifts will make room for us. Mignon is using her gifts to make room for herself and has built an empire doing so. Her story of triumph in the face of defeat and her roadmap for those in similar straights are her gifts to you, the reader.

Made from Scratch: Finding Success Without a Recipe is a testimony of resilience. If you chop the same tree every day, three or four times a day for thousands of days in a row—that consistency and the predictability of the outcome are the blueprint that Mignon's book lays out. *Made from Scratch* demonstrates that it's possible to get from the bottom to the top, even when it seems everything is working against you.

That's why I can't endorse this book enough and I am over the moon that Mignon chose me to provide the foreword. *Made from Scratch* is a story I want my daughter and your daughters to read, and I will gladly share its message with those I meet and mentor. Her story is universal and broadly applicable. Mignon's life, as she tells it here, including the ups and downs, will encourage and give hope to anyone, but especially women at their wits' end.

I can shout from the mountaintop that *Made from Scratch* is a literary contribution that will provide a touchstone for anyone who feels that they've come to the end of their rope. After reading Mignon's story, they'll discover that what seems like an ending can be the beginning of a beautiful journey.

Mignon's story, as told here, perfectly epitomizes Romans 8:28—that all things work together for the good of them that love the Lord and are called according to His purpose.

I'm so proud of Mignon for her accomplishments and for sharing her story. Mignon may never know how many lives have been touched and changed because she shared her journey in this book, but I know her words will not return void. I can't wait to see the harvest yielded from the people who heeded her lessons, applied the wisdom gleaned from her experiences, and used them to transform and transition from where they are to where our God would have them to be!

Eric Thomas, PhD
Author, Pastor, Educator, Motivational Speaker
Co-host, *The Secret to Success* Podcast

Count It All Joy!

Count it all joy when you face
trials of many kinds because you
know that the testing of your
faith develops perseverance.
Perseverance must finish its work
so that you may be mature and
complete not lacking anything.

(James 1:2–4, NIV)

Introduction

Who told you to go make cupcakes?

was never supposed to be here. I am everything a girl was not supposed to be in order to be successful: I got married too young, I had a baby way too early, and despite all the preparation my parents gave me, I ended up on welfare, food stamps, at risk of losing everything while living in the dark, on the verge of foreclosure, and scraping coins from the couch to buy red beans and potatoes or gas for the car to take my children to school.

To hear my story might in the beginning sound like a pity party for one. Can you imagine that announcement coming from the hostess stand in a crowded restaurant?

"Mignon? Pity Party of One, your table is now available."

Who would want a seat at that table or get an invitation to that party? Not me, even though that was indeed my life. But no matter how I felt, I got it on the inside of me to never allow myself to look like what I was going through. I decided that if God's promises are the real deal, then no matter what my situation looked like, everything happening to me was actually happening for me (Romans 8:28). I used my smile to increase my face value, even if I held nothing else of worth in my possession.

Yet soon after I started on this journey, God let me know I did have something of value, a treasure He would reveal in my name. Knowing that, I decided to always smile like everybody was watching, even if I was starting over from scratch, with scratch, on the scratch line.

The journey, however, has not been easy or without stumbles or mistakes—or people who helped along the way. But I never gave up and when I finally set out to make and sell cupcakes, I did the first thing I knew to do if I wanted to accomplish anything remotely good in the kitchen. I called my grandma, a robust, joyful woman who lived on Bayou Black, a 66.6-mile-long river in Texas and Louisiana, just outside Houma, Louisiana.

When I got her recipe right, I did the next thing I knew to do-- just what she would have done. I gave them away.

I didn't have a plan for what it would take to turn my cupcakes, or any other businesses I began, into a viable venture. I hadn't set my sights on that. Field trip money! That's all I really wanted deep down, and maybe the promise of helping out with the utilities every now and then so that never again would my children flip a light switch that did not respond. I expected nothing more than the proceeds an old-fashioned schoolhouse bake sale could have garnered. I just did it like I've done most things--flying by the seat of my pants.

And by the time that bake sale began growing into a thriving bakery business, I still didn't have a clue.

Here is what I knew—that in the wee hours of the morning, God was waking me up. He wanted to spend time with me and share an idea that He had in store for me. With every waking day, I wrote every nagging or fleeting thought I heard in those morning meetups with God. I tucked them in a 5"x7" journal that I had been gifted by my friend, Catherine. A bona fide prayer warrior and ordained bishop, Catherine had sent me the journal book twenty years earlier, urging me to write my prayers to God. The reason? So that when

He answered, I would know what to thank Him for, what not to complain about because I had asked for it, and what praise reports to offer in response to the prayers that didn't get answered or for the ones to which He flat out said no.

This book unfolds the collective of the prayers I wrote to God, the answers He provided, and the story behind it all—from quieting the noise in my life to asking Him to give me a product I could sell to make money. Never mind that He had given me products and services that I had set aside because, honestly, I was just too afraid to see them to fruition.

I didn't have a manual. I didn't have a manuscript. I didn't even have a viable written recipe to start with. What I did have was a promise from God that He would make me successful and an assurance that other people would also get on their knees, formulate prayers, and ask Him to make me successful. In those waking hours of the day, God told me to make cupcakes, and everything that went along with it— from the name of the business to how He would bless it.

The catch? I had to trust and obey Him, no matter what the circumstances looked like.

Let me tell you this, when God knocks on the door of your consciousness and says, "Come sit down and let Me talk to you," it can be a scary thing. When I showed up to hear from God, I literally asked Him not to talk to me. Waiting for His voice to fill the room is terrifying at best. But when He finally does speak to you, when you finally recognize how He speaks, it will be reassuring and familiar.

On the journey from there to here, God has been faithful to His promise. As you prepare to crack open this story, know that the words therein are my effort to be faithful to Him in keeping mine, so that no matter where you are in the world, I Am (God in you) there to tell you that all you have is everything you need. No matter what time it is when the feeling strikes or the need arises, I Am there to remind you to look for the lesson. No matter where I Am, it will

3

always be the exact right place to tell you that joy comes in the m-o-u-r-n-i-n-g. But the key is that joy comes.

What I am about to share is personal; some of it I've never shared publicly. But I promised God that if He would make me successful, I would tell anyone who would listen about what they could do if they believe.

So here it goes....

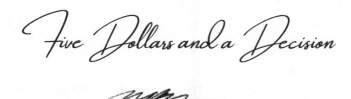

Five Dollars and a Decision

"Don't let adverse facts stand in the way of a good decision."
~ Gen. Colin Powell

Who could be knocking at our door? No one ever used that verdigris copper door knocker. Attached to the reddish orange door of our plum purple painted brick home hung a pineapple stained a greenish patina from the elements and lack of use. It was a beloved piece I had purchased from Restoration Hardware many years before we ever had a permanent door to hang it on. It was a substantially heavy piece that, when used properly, could send a sound wave through the house making me think maybe the police were at the door.

I love that pineapple. I saved it for years, carrying it from place to place believing that one day we would find our forever home. It graces our door as a symbol of hospitality to welcome guests or be a warning signal that unwanted or unannounced visitors had beckoned. I never wanted to affix it to the places that I knew were temporary. That pineapple became my symbol of hope that one day we would have a stable home life and be settled.

We now had that home. But keeping it remained a struggle, and now the sound of knocking was so intrusive that I nearly jumped out of my skin. My heart felt as if it were pounding out of my chest.

5

Who does that? Who knocks on someone's door like that midday? In broad daylight? Forget all that stuff about pineapples and hospitality, I wasn't feeling it that day.

Because of our unstable circumstances, whenever someone came to the door, I was on guard for the looming trauma that might await me on the other side. I tiptoed quietly toward the door. I did not want to blow my cover just in case I needed to pretend no one was home. I was careful to cling to the wall as I inched toward the door. The huge peephole we had installed in the front door—about the size of a small child's palm—didn't exactly provide cover from visitors who were curious enough to peep in here. As I made my gradual approach toward the door, I could see it was Joanie, my neighbor who had grown up around Nashville and had the accent to prove it. She and her husband loved our family dearly. They had no children and had vested themselves in the lives of the six Black children who had begun to color the neighborhood and their lives from across Sixth Avenue.

Joanie had grown impatient with my slow approach toward the door in stealth mode. She peered through that humongous peephole. "Mignon," she sang out in a perfectly pitched French pronunciation of my name. "I know you're in there."

I flung the door open and pasted on a smile to greet her. "Hey, Joanie."

"Are you busy?" She was excited about something I could tell. She had been cooking up something, and she just knew I was going to love it.

I thought she hadn't noticed that I let that first inquisition soar straight over my head and land somewhere in the darkness that was my backdrop. She peered past me into the dark shadows of the 50-foot hallway behind me. She noticed! She always notices! And she doesn't hesitate to ask the questions that she wants and expects answers to.

"Why are you in the dark?" Joanie's thick southern accent made her inquisitions seem innocent and nosey at the same time.

"I'm meditating," I said, fidgeting around in my mind for the next answer if she asked me even one thing about that.

I was not about to tell her that we had no electricity and that I was sitting in the dark because I had no better option at the moment. Gratefully, Joanie was satisfied with my response, and she proceeded to tell me her thoughts.

The Christmas holidays were approaching, and Joanie had come up with the brilliant idea to buy cupcakes for all her clients as thank-you gifts for the season. She absolutely loves the holiday season, and everything associated with it—decorating, gift giving, and being the one to introduce her friends to what she believed was the best kept secret in Nashville. Lemon was one of her favorite flavors. How do I know that? She turned us onto some amazing lemon cookies from a local place in town. When we wanted lemon cookies, she would get them for us. When we asked where they came from so that we could buy some without feeling like beggars, she would brush over the request and reply, "Oh, I'll get them for you whenever you want them."

But she also knew my gift for lemon—and had sampled my lemon cupcakes. Now there was a new lemon queen in town, she wanted everybody to get a taste of Mignon's baking. Between Joanie and the rest of our Germantown neighbors, our "lemon drop" cupcakes were growing in popularity and our home had been coined the "lemon crack house." She, along with the rest of the neighborhood, was hooked.

So, naturally, she wanted lemon cupcakes—six hundred of them to be exact.

Locking her hands together and wringing them with excitement, Joanie's face was overcome with joy that she could bring me an order like this. She loved the idea.

I didn't.

Truthfully, had Joanie known what she was walking into, her brilliant idea to help build my dream of a cupcake business would have seemed more like a nightmare.

Unsure how I could pull off such a tall request, I began calculating coins in my head as I tried to reconcile whether or not I could fill her order. In the middle of my mental calculations, I also began contemplating all the ways she might wait to pay my invoice. And if I said yes to her offer, right now, today, that would be a large gamble.

My mind wandered from the room and whatever Joanie was saying to figure out how this was going to happen.

"You hate it!" Joanie said, becoming deflated as she was scanning my face for any indication of excitement over an order that could change the holidays for my household.

What Joanie didn't know was that at the same time she was inspired to wander across the street and knock on our door, I had been sitting in the back of my house negotiating how to make the best use of the five-dollar bill I had on the table. I had been opening containers and pulling back the curtains that served as makeshift doors on my kitchen cabinets. The cheerful pattern of red and green apples was my frugal attempt to mask our lack of ability to build a kitchen as a French country cottage design feature. If the cobbler's children have no shoes, the custom cabinet maker's wife has no cupboard doors. And God bless the children of the general contractor—well, they have no paint on their walls, no covering on the floors, and their rooms don't have doors.

"What's wrong?" she asked, drawing my attention back. Without waiting for a response, she blurted, "Tell you what...as you make them, I'll pay you."

She had read the distress on my face and must have figured out why I wasn't exactly wowed about an order for six hundred cupcakes. I've always been transparent in my personality. She read the questions competing loudly inside my head. Who's supposed to pay for this? If I'm going to sacrifice our family's food money, we have one shot to get it in before all the money is depleted.

Joanie and I are from different places. She being from the privilege of the 1960s American Dream, and me being a product of the Jim Crow South. When she said pay as you go, she quietly meant when I got around to it.

"So, I can make you a few today, get paid, and then make some more?" I confirmed her offer.

I went back to my mental calculations of the five dollars I had and what it could do if she paid me as she proposed. At the same time, ever cautious of our family's limited resources, I wagered in my mind what would happen if she didn't.

I had five dollars and a decision to make—keep the sure thing that would provide us dinner for a week or take a gamble and possibly feed the family for the rest of the month. Granted, five dollars wasn't much to buy groceries back in 2007, but I was going to figure out how to make it happen. I always did, by the grace of God, and we didn't go hungry.

As I considered my options, I realized that five dollars was enough to buy ingredients to make the first batch of cupcakes. I've heard it said that when you're down to nothing, God is up to something. I couldn't see anything God might be up to at the time, but He was definitely at work in my life that sunny late fall day in Nashville.

"Okay! I'll do it," I gave her the smile she had hoped for in the beginning. And when she walked back down my steps and across the street, she promenaded home.

I closed the door, not completely sure of what I had just convinced her that I could do. But I had been listening to a man on the radio telling people to have a bake sale to get out of debt. He hadn't been wrong yet, and that's when I had a come-to-Jesus conversation with heaven.

Back in the kitchen where I had been meditating over the chaos in our lives, I started on my plan, working by the flicker of sun forcing its way through the tiny window. Dave Ramsey, the man I had been listening to on the radio, was teaching people how to get out of debt using an envelope system he called the "baby step plan." My husband was not one to cash his paychecks and bring them to me to manage our household affairs. He brought me whatever was left after he had done whatever he wanted to do. It was up to me to figure out how to make do with what remained.

So, I learned to work with what I was given and to save the bits of income even if I had to piece it together. I would tuck the money into individual envelopes with a plan of collecting enough by month's end to pay bills with what I could gather. I would then hide the envelopes away where only I could discover them—twenty for this bill, one hundred for that one. Listening to that radio show, I had learned the importance of securing "our four walls" first: food, utilities, housing, and transportation. Having done as much as I could with what I had, which unfortunately didn't include paying the electric bill, I was left with five dollars. Nothing was secured for the month, and I had no indication of when any more money was coming.

Digging in those cabinets, I inventoried a large vat of rice that we kept on hand, some potatoes, and a plethora of dried seasonings. Add in a little cornmeal and flour—I was busy deciding how I was going to make this money stretch into meals. I'm a New Orleans girl at the core. Red beans and rice, that's what's for dinner. Not just tonight. I could hear my children's groans already. Every night. I would make it work, though. I can make a mean batch of cornbread and sprinkle in Ramen noodles here and there to break up the monotony.

"Are you there, God? It's me, Mignon. Why would you give me an opportunity so large when I don't even have the money to take it? It's either this order or our dinner."

"I feed birds," I heard God say as clearly and distinctly as a literal voice in the room. "They don't toil or store up in barns. I clothe the lilies in all their splendor that are here today and gone tomorrow. How much more will I take care of you who looks like me?" (See Matthew 6:26–34).

I could have brought up other issues in that moment, but I decided to take God at His word and leave it there. I chose not to focus on the fact that our north Nashville home, although it was in a trending up-and-coming community known as Germantown, was being run from a generator that my husband had brought home from a construction site where, yet again, he was either overworked, underpaid, or had over promised.

Me? I was over it! I had just heard God say, "I got you, Mignon." We didn't have the money to turn our electricity back on, so while my husband was out earning cash to pay the light bill, I was busy trying something different. But I wasn't just trying something new for that day. I wanted life for my children, one filled with the abundance their peers knew so intimately. We would crank up the generator at night to give them light and hot water, but I wanted a day when they could simply flick the light switch at any time on any day, and the electricity would respond. I wanted water for them that ran from the faucets and not from gallon jugs schlepped home from the neighborhood store and heated by a flame for warm baths. I wanted my children not to choose between a freezing cold shower or sharing tub water with a dirty little brother or sister who had a habit of bed wetting. I had been trying hard to make their lives as normal as possible, so I would sit in the dark during the day and work by the light of one of the large windows in our historic home.

That was my simple and earnest dream for our children. Meanwhile, for today, it was game on!

I laced up my shoes and marched to the nearby supermarket with five dollars in my hand and destiny at my feet, not knowing this was about to be the day my life and my perspective would change. I bought all the ingredients for the order I could with those five dollars, and Joanie bought all that I could make that very day, just like she said. I had been sitting in a dark kitchen that morning with my last five dollars, but by the day's end, five dollars had turned into sixty dollars. And by the end of the week, that sixty dollars had become six hundred dollars.

And just like when Annie in the *Little Orphan Annie* movie moved in with Daddy Warbucks, I could feel myself inspired to burst into song. And even though the curtain never lifted for that monumental number, I did think I was going to like it here.

A house without electricity, a propane-powered stove, and five dollars to buy ingredients to make six hundred cupcakes was not the ideal way to start a business, but with that six hundred dollars in my hands, by the end of that week I was encouraged to believe more was possible for our family. I've always been a person of faith. It defines my being, but now I had tangible evidence that my current circumstances did not have to frame my future.

"Bakery Coming Soon." I dared to make a sign and hang it from our front porch railing.

Bakery Coming, Just Not Soon

"Find out what you like doing best and get someone to pay you for doing it." ~ Katherine Whitehorn

When I put up that sign, I was a stay-at-home wife and mother of six, deeply in debt, and trying to hold my family together in a marriage that was sliding further and further into the abyss. Meanwhile, I was always looking for some way to motivate my husband to follow my lead, but to little avail. Although I knew I had what it took to succeed, and I knew he had the skill, by the time I put that sign out, I knew if any business endeavor I launched was going to be successful, I would have to go after it alone.

Our daughter Lauren would be graduating from high school soon, and I wanted to afford the expenses that came with her senior year, including prom, class dues, and senior trip. I knew if I didn't do something, she was going to be let down at the last minute. I was really tired of those last-minute letdowns and pawning our belongings to pull through.

By putting up the sign, I knew it would push me to follow through. The bakery didn't exactly come soon. Eventually I got it open, but the grand opening of a separate location would be no less than two years in the making. In the meantime, I worked at The Cupcake

Collection—the name my family had chosen for our home-based business—like it was my job. Word-of-mouth advertising worked in my favor, so I pretty much worked like I already had it open—trying new recipes and using my family as taste testers.

I had gotten a lot of business experience inadvertently along the way because of our rather flimsy family finances; I was always starting a business or thinking a little about business. My husband had started a lot of side businesses through which I learned how to start, conduct, and manage the responsibilities that come with entrepreneurship. I'd always maintain faith that one day he would get it together with one of his business ventures. So, I was always just looking for a way to help, either through a side hustle or outside employment.

In those years I had plenty of business ideas and had several startups—making wedding veils, creating custom baby books, and taking wedding photographs. I started making custom baby books in 1993, designing custom wedding veils in 1996, and taking wedding photographs in 1999. The problem? I was an expert at starting, but I just didn't know how to either make it stick or make me stick to it. Yet I don't count those startups as a waste of time. I learned certain elements of running a business that would come to serve me well no matter what the venture turned out to be.

Nevertheless, because my business startups were just that, startups, I was always looking for a job that could provide. I remember applying for a job at FedEx while we lived in Houston. I did it online using dial-up Internet in our two-bedroom apartment. I was seeking a package handler or a customer-service position in the call center. The customer service job was more within my skillset but required typing. I wasn't a fast typist, but I passed the test for consideration. The human resources rep told me to expect a call back within a couple of days to schedule my start date. I was super excited about this job, confidently believing that this could be a ticket to real change in our lives.

By the weekend, our phone had been disconnected.

I tried my best to get our telephone service back on right away. One call to the phone company revealed that this wasn't going to happen quickly. I owed way too much, had way too little money, and by now they were catching on that I had a habit of running up large phone bills that took way too long to pay. I even called the local FedEx office from a pay phone, which was like my second line, figuring that I could find the responsible party who could give me the instructions I so desperately needed to lead me to work. All I could get was a recording, but I left the number to the payphone and my mother's home number in New Orleans for someone to reach out to me. I waited for a call that never came and watched the mail for a letter that never arrived. It would be some time before I did land a job, but when I did it was a good one.

I had been raised by parents who had stayed at the same company for 35 years. They had climbed their respective corporate ladders and made a good name for our family as hard workers. My mother worked at MetLife, an insurance company, and my father and stepmother worked for Bellsouth, the mother of landline telephone companies. By the time I sought employment there, BellSouth had again merged with AT&T. Going to BellSouth/AT&T in Houston seeking employment felt like asking a family friend for a job. I landed an interview, and when asked why I wanted to work for the conglomeration, I beamed, knowing its values because my father had worked there my entire life. It was an easy yes for the company to take me on, and I didn't even have to wait for a phone call. I was super excited to inform my dad, who had so many questions about what I would be doing. He didn't return my excitement about me following his footsteps, which was a little disappointing, but I knew he was proud. I'll never know why he didn't display more enthusiasm over my new job. Maybe he wanted more for me than spending a lifetime at the telephone company.

My acceptance letter from AT&T arrived by mail, listing all the details about my job. Employee training would begin with the next customer service representative class. On my first day of employee training, I pulled up to a concrete building in front of an unmarked door armed only with my packed lunch. My very basic lunch included a sandwich made with thinly sliced, prepackaged deli turkey on bargain brand white bread that would become slightly soggy from the slice of tomato and lettuce, salvaged only by the barrier of cheese I had slipped between the layers. I also had a Thermos with my drink, and a few tightly packed potato chips that I'd squeezed into a Ziploc bag. All of this was tucked into the fabric lunchbox that I had meticulously selected from Walmart. I was proud of me.

I loved working in the AT&T call center, and I eventually managed to get on one of the top-producing sales teams. I felt accomplished and independent. I made my highly competitive manager very proud. Shelita—a beautifully warm brown motherly type, the color of red mahogany with dark black hair positioned perfectly in its place—was a competitive leader. I'm not sure how old she was; the only crack on her face was through the smile she flashed to show snowy white teeth that literally blinged when she smiled. I made sales goals and kept in step with her team as her newest adoptee. Shelita was a winner and coming to her team meant I needed to be a winner, too. I always have had a competitive edge and a desire to win. When our training class visited the sales floor for live call training, I scoped the landscape for the team I wanted to join.

Shelita Adams' team was rowdy but professional, and she loved each member. The team's area was decorated with balloons to celebrate their sales accomplishments for the week, and Shelita's desk was covered with casseroles and cakes she'd made to inspire their commitment to keep succeeding. I wanted to work for her. I wanted to be with those winners. I guess the managers had some say as to which trainees they would take on, and I was nervous that I would be placed with a team that was not as accomplished.

When I graduated from training, I landed on the team right next to Shelita's. Ughhh! I didn't want to be there and made it known that I wanted to be on her team. From time to time, she would flash a pearly white smile over at me and watch how I was progressing. I don't know exactly how it happened or when, but one day I got moved to her winning team. Being a player on the champion team was a dream come true. The winners got prizes and certificates that could be used at affiliated companies to make purchases. I used my first certificate at JC Penney to buy some plush cotton towels for my linen closet and sheets for my children's twin beds.

My desk chair was often covered in balloons for meeting whatever goals our manager had set—like selling additional phone lines, accessory packages, or new customer lines. I was having a blast making my own money and coming into my own stride, working to provide. While I was enjoying the ride, I spied what I wanted next—a management seat. I didn't want to just work for Shelita. I wanted to be like Shelita. I asked my team leader for the manual to begin mapping the steps to management and her blessing when I got the call from the railyard. "Your husband has been hurt on the job," the caller said. All I remember is dropping the phone and looking into my manager's concerned eyes. I kept mine fixed on hers, searching back and forth, left and right, looking for answers of what to do now.

My husband, who also was employed in a legacy position with Southern Pacific Railroad, had been working in one of the rail cars. He was fixing an electrical issue just before quitting time, when someone accidentally released a chemical substance into the air, unaware that he was in there. It knocked him out and greatly impacted his capacity to breathe for more than a year.

I had to quit the job I so dearly loved to take care of him. I really didn't want to leave that job, and I cried over my loss. Looking back, that's what I really loved, not so much the job, but the feeling I got from having it. Even more, I think I mourned the opportunity to have a life that I had just gotten started building, one with economic independence, sprinkled with some frivolous and innocuous opportunity.

God was with us, though. Even without my income, our family was able to survive off payments he received from the railroad company. Still, I missed the career I had been building through AT&T.

His road to recovery was long, but I nursed my husband back from the consequences of his accident that day in the railyard. He learned to breathe through asthmatic lungs while I learned to juggle being sole provider and caregiver.

It's funny how what seems to be the worst thing in the moment can end up being the best thing for your future. At first, I was extremely disappointed that I didn't get that job at FedEx; turns out, though, I never really wanted that. A package handler? Really, Mignon? I was never going to survive the conditions of throwing packages in a non-air-conditioned environment during peak hours of the day. Perhaps if I had explored the options with more clarity and detail, I could have decided on a position I deemed worth having and applied for one I could be satisfied with. What I did get, though, was some practice. The hiring process at FedEx prepared me for the job I landed at AT&T. I practiced my typing skills in those coveted quiet hours while my children napped, and I raised my words per minute to a level that made me a shoo-in for the job.

The AT&T job planted me in a legacy position within the company that my father and stepmother had spent more than three decades serving. That job taught me training by manuals and the value of creating a process. The experience also taught me what it means to give top-notch customer service. I learned the value of communicating with customers, and a technique they taught me all those years ago is one I use in training my customer-service teams today.

Standing in the middle of the massive sales floor, the AT&T trainer addressed what must have been a few hundred team members.

"I want you to close your eyes for sixty seconds," he instructed, "and then open them when you think time is up." It seemed like such a long time. Some opened their eyes after only fifteen or twenty seconds in. What he showed us is that a minute is a really long time, especially when you're waiting in silence. The point was that when people are put on hold for a minute, the customer service rep needs to check back. That training taught me to be mindful of when a customer is waiting, whether on the phone or at the counter. They want to know what is going on, so you connect back to update them, "Hey, I'm still working on that," or "Can I take your telephone number and call you back? This is taking me longer than expected." People value their time and appreciate it when others do, too. They don't want to wait, especially if they're holding with nothing to fill that space, like music. Extensive periods of call waiting can make the customer feel the company has disregarded the value of their time.

The waiting customer usually can't see what's going on in the background. All they know is, "I have been on hold for five whole minutes," and it probably feels much longer in the moment. I learned to tell them what's going on and say, "I'm working on it." It's a way of reassuring them that they matter and their patronage matters. This is something I teach my team at The Cupcake Collection, and that has made us excel in customer service. It's just good business: We may not have the answer right now, but we keep people informed, and that makes it so much easier for them to deal with the wait.

The same thing is true for life in general. In life, if you know what's coming, you can deal with it, at least for a little while. I always know that I can handle whatever life throws at me because God doesn't give me anything I cannot handle. But in life, childbirth, and in customer service, we can do hard things—at least for a little while—and that's what I learned at AT&T.

While my time there was cut short due to my husband's accident, something bigger grew out of the opportunity—becoming a college graduate. In 1999, I earned my bachelor of science degree from Houston Baptist University, with a dual major in mass media and psychology, culminating more than nine years of coursework to get to graduation. I'd always been a fast learner and had graduated first in my high school class, and even tested out in the eleventh grade. But the precarious nature of our finances routed me on a nine-year journey to earn a four-year degree and an equivalent master's degree from the school of hard knocks.

While I was pursuing my degree, I got an unpaid internship at the local newspaper in Katy, Texas. I worked the "slice of life" beat, writing stories about fun things going on in the small town. I wrote stories, took pictures, and learned a lot from my supervisor, a thin blonde lady who had been in the business a long time, to whom I owe a lot of the savvy I enjoyed as an assignment reporter. Later, I interned at a photography studio, which helped me to hone my skills and sharpen my eye as a photographer. Theirs was a studio steeped in marketing and advertising experience, specifically in food photography. I worked with food stylists and brand specialists on product shots that made it to the grocery store shelves. The small group of owner-operators were all folks whose names started with M and having lost one of the Ms to raising her family, they offered me a permanent position, which I ultimately had to refuse. I was still taking care of a recovering husband and was there to glean what I could to get me to graduation.

Since neither internship came with compensation, I didn't get an opportunity to reap all that they could've meant for me. I was a good writer and a promising photographer, but eventually, I needed to make some money. Still, working those two internships gave me the practice behind the lens and the keyboard I would need to later be my own marketing and content creator for the first several years at The Cupcake Collection—my passion project and the most improbable place for my ultimate success.

After graduation, I pondered what would be next. We had been living in Houston for five years when a night terror woke me, and I screamed for my husband. Wiping the sleep from his eyes and wondering what the heck I was doing up, dressing and throwing clothes in an overnight bag, he struggled to come up to speed with my energy and why our children were being wrapped in blankets and being packed for the car.

Actual tears were streaming down my face. Moments earlier I had been encased in a vision, standing on the outside of a coffin with my mother resting inside. That was a nightmare, but in real life, I had watched my mother lose every one of her immediate family members between the ages of forty and forty-nine, with the most recent being my uncle, Jimmy. At age forty-nine, she had been experiencing some unexplained issues with her health. That vision, for me, was the only warning I needed to get into gear.

"You can stay here if you want," I told him. Desperation to see my mother alive fueled me to drive all night from Houston to Atlanta, stopping only once for gas. I had already packed his things as well, so he filed into the car and followed suit.

Not long after the visit to my mother, we relocated to Atlanta to be closer to family and more opportunity. More of the same seemed to plague us there; that is, until a golden opportunity presented itself—a job in my field in The Home Depot's communications department. I had struggled to get a job in my field for so long, and I finally landed a good one that I loved.

I started working as a cashier at The Home Depot as a way to make ends meet and to have adult conversation. The store I applied to was just at the top of the hill from the apartment that we had rented in Lawrenceville, Georgia, a suburb northeast of Atlanta. Mostly, though, I was there to earn daycare money for my then 4-year-old daughter, who was eager to get me to work so that she could go to school. She walked with me up that steep, long climb to the Big Box orange store with no complaints, obliged to help me fill out the application at the hiring kiosk if that meant she could go to school like she had seen her brothers do.

My baby, Brittany, was enrolled in pre-K, and I was feeling as if I was finally about to get my own life. That girl was so smart. From an early age, she loved reading so much more than I wanted to read to her. Drawing from the experience I gained babysitting another eager reader like her during my teen years, I recorded myself reading her favorite books. The recordings made a chiming sound when it was time for her to turn the page. I didn't have the money to purchase professionally produced books on tape; besides, she wanted to hear her mommy's voice reading to her. She got so good with those tapes in her little tape player that she began recognizing the words. She could sight-read about one hundred words by the time she was three years old.

"Mommy, you need to get a job, because I want to go to school."

So, that's what I did. I got a job, the first one I could find that didn't require a car to get to and wouldn't require a long hiring process, just in case the phones weren't working in my favor.

But the weeks-long training for that position was in Stone Mountain—thirty-two miles away. In Atlanta, often referred to as "the ATL," that could easily be a fifty-five-minute drive each way, and that was on a good day. "I can do anything for a little while," I remembered. So, I took the job as a cashier making ten dollars an hour. It wasn't what I had expected, but I was grateful. I hadn't planned to be in that position long, but even if God had other plans, that was more money than I had made for any significant amount of time in the span of...ever.

Fresh out of school and on the hunt for a big break, I had bigger plans than staying at the local store level working behind the register for long. I had this idea that if I started from scratch in a really large company the same way that my parents did, I could climb the corporate ladder. I was right. While I was there, I often saw postings for corporate jobs within the company's headquarters in the suburban community of Smyrna, which was more than thirty-five miles from where we lived. I wasted no time picking through jobs I might qualify for, and even though I had only been on the store team for a few months, I landed a position as a writer in the communications department at headquarters.

Interviewing internally proved to be so much easier than starting as an outsider. I knew I had that job in the bag, and this time I wouldn't have to wait on a phone call to tell me so. Having finished the writing test faster than she had imagined, I walked over to the director of communications' office to turn in my test and thank her for the opportunity. Her back was turned to the door and she was peering through a huge window into the Atlanta sky. She was busy on the phone, talking about this young talented writer she had just interviewed and who she thought was perfect for the position. I listened and waited, hoping that I was the fresh young talent she was talking about. We both were caught off guard and a little embarrassed when she turned around to see me standing there, but that embarrassment soon turned into an open door to communicate salary and a start date.

I would be overseeing "Doings at the Depot," an internal publication that celebrated the accomplishments and milestones of store associates. I had to plan and execute ideas for the cover, working alongside a graphic designer who found my giant grin, my prayer-is-the-answer-to-everything outlook, and my positive spin on life to be annoying. In addition to learning the value of content collaboration, conflict resolution, and a heavy dose of prayer in the office, I learned a lot about who I wanted to be in the workplace. I sat at a desk next to that graphic designer every month when she and I "put the paper to bed," a term used to signify the closing of a publication before printing.

I took that publication very seriously. It was important to me, and I applied the journalistic skills I had learned in school, at the

Katy Times, and at that photography studio run by friends. Together we turned it into a quality journalistic publication. The director of communications had a vision for the publication, and under her leadership we won our first journalistic award in the history of the publication that year.

Everything I had done before that time had prepared me for that position. What I didn't know then was how that job would also prepare me for what was to come.

God's Promises Don't Expire

"Ideas have a short shelf life. You must act on them before the expiration date." ~ John C. Maxwell

My head was pounding. It was one of those throbbings, that tap-tap-tap at the center of your skull, like whatever was on the inside was seeking attention from the outside. Tiny little squirming floaters took over the spans of my eyesight as my vision started to blur. I pulled into a supermarket parking lot in search of nourishment. Moments later, I emerged from the grocery store armed with a salad for dinner and a candy bar for my reward.

Side Note: I eat a lot of salad. Mind you, eating salad is not making me skinnier, but perhaps I don't know that yet. It's colorful, dynamic, and textured. Like pentameter in a song, salad has crunch, bitterness, and bold color. Attitude, drama, and depth from a feast curated of radicchio, endive, Batavia, frisée, or mâche. My children are mostly grown now and feeding me is pretty much the highest selfish act I perform in any day. Either I'm bored or unimaginative in the space of my own nourishment. Even in the place where anything can be made to come to life, I get pre-chopped, bagged iceberg lettuce in a bag—satisfied to cut into it and dump the contents into one large bowl.

As I came out of the store, I saw what looked like a four-door 1995 Toyota Tercel. I peered at the car's washed-out color. "Wait.

This is a time machine." I mean, it might as well have been a time machine as I was frozen still. But in my imagination, I traveled down memory lane back to Houston, to a time I really wanted that car.

Actually, I remember a time when I wanted anything from God. I wanted answers to prayers, money in the bank, healthy children, safety from harm, serenity, and wisdom to know the difference. I wanted to stay at home with my children and be a serial entrepreneur. I wanted to finish my college degree and have a closer walk with Jesus. I wanted to live out my dreams and have dinner on the table every night without having to buy my groceries with Food Stamps. Sometimes I wished for Food Stamps, though, but only because that meant—food. Newsflash, you cannot get Food Stamps just because you need them. I wanted a loving marriage and at times I wanted a divorce. I wanted to know where I was going, and I wanted to be there when I arrived. I wanted to lose weight. I still want to lose weight. I wanted to be successful. I wanted independence. I wanted to make my parents proud.

Of all the things I was asking for, it was like going to the grocery store hungry. I wasn't asking from a place of longing or purpose. I was asking because I was tired, jaded, bored, and fed up.

But when we'd first moved to Houston, we quickly learned that one of the biggest needs of any resident there was transportation. Houston is huge, in both land mass and population. Plus, Houston was five hours away from my family in New Orleans. My husband worked outside of the home, and my job was to work inside of it. That's the way it felt. No buses or mass transportation were available and getting to anywhere required a car or at least a network of friends to link up with and travel about. Getting to the grocery store, which was less than a mile away, also required transportation because crossing busy four-lane highways was like playing the video game Frogger with your life, avoiding trucks, taxis, and bicyclists with baby Brittany in a stroller, toddler Dillon holding one hand, and third grader Alexius in tow. The Texans called these highways "farm-to-market roads." The very name farm-to-market road suggests dodging tractor-trailers. At least in the video game, you got extra points if you made it home safely.

The Tercel I wanted was an incredibly small car, hardly a thing that could fit my growing family for the long commutes around Houston. A simple drive around the city could take as much as an hour, even with no traffic, using the Texas Beltway 8, an eighty-eight-mile loop in Harris County where we lived. Everything in Texas was big to me, except maybe this dream car I wanted. I had a long-legged third grader, a preschooler who ranked in the ninety-fifth percentile by height but was still in a car seat, and a new baby girl in an infant carrier—all of which needed to fit in the back seat. If I had put those two car seats in the back of that compact car, my eldest would have literally been smashed between the two. Plus, when I was asking God for it, I never imagined what my six-foot, two-hundred-plus pound husband would look like attempting to drive it and be even remotely comfortable. What would he look like in Houston traffic? Squoozen…and yes, I intended to use that word for "squeezed," which doesn't draw the visual of him stuffed in the compact car's metal frame.

But I was desperate for reliable transportation. I made all kinds of deals with God, desperately seeking whatever I thought I needed for today. On this day it would be a prayer for a car. "God, if you would just give me a car…"

Stranded! Just writing that word on the page feels like a ship wrecking, running aground, but hardly a big enough word to describe how we often had no way to get around the city. We lived in areas where you had to have a car to negotiate your surroundings. My cars were always a thorn in my side. Transportation has been crucial for me, and I have had to fight for every car I ever got and subsequently fight to keep it.

Transportation, according to *Britannica.com*, can basically be defined as the movement of persons from place to place, and the success by which it can be accomplished on a grand scale effectively has long been an index for the viability of a city. Why? Because what doesn't move, dies. It's like stagnant water. A confined body of water with no flow often has an unpleasant smell that attracts mosquitoes to nest—pests that have one main job: sucking the life-carrying blood out of its host.

I had to get moving. And I had to get my kids moving.

To a woman who feels stuck, a car is a symbol of freedom. At least a dependable car offered options I could control. Emphasis on the word dependable. With no way to get around, I felt trapped in the house, under arrest and unable to do anything with or about my own life until someone could collect me and my children. Maybe I viewed it as a status symbol—that I feel it's an accomplishment to have a nice car. Maybe it's something that has been important in my family because my parents have always had nice cars and it's something they instilled in me. I don't know where that comes from. Maybe it's because I was always struggling for things, and when I was married especially, we were always living way beyond our means.

At first, I wanted God to make it possible for me to have a brand-new car. But looking back, I had begged God for a tiny car to somehow get me from point A to point B that might be great on gas but horrible at accomplishing the task of carting around my husband, myself, and our three children, not to mention room for the other two respectively placed "stair steps" if they came to visit.

I never got that Tercel. What I got instead was a 1972 "ocean liner," a four-door, limited-edition Cadillac Fleetwood Brougham my husband called Nellie. It wasn't pretty or new, but it worked, and as I drove it across Houston, I began to ask God again, because this time, I had a new dream car in mind....a Volvo.

I had believed the ads, and in my mind, the best car to want as a respectable mom who loved her children was a Volvo. The company had introduced the XC90, a mid-size luxury SUV, a modern take on the minivan. I felt like someone had gone inside of my head. All my visits to the car dealer, asking why something like this doesn't exist, were finally paying off. Could it be that "Big Brother" does listen well after all?

This model had buttery-tan leather seats, complete with a built-in booster seat that could be customized to replace an infant car seat—the one that normally rides in the car but is currently in your own mom's car because she was going to pick up the baby from preschool. That, however, was before you forgot that the school was dismissing early, and Mom was on the other side of town in her water aerobics class she refused to miss for your lack of planning.

Having this car would let me be hip, stylish, and practical while not looking like a soccer mom. I wanted to be the soccer mom, I just didn't want to look like a soccer mom, especially not the one in oversized gray sweatpants with unkempt hair managing the car pick-up and drop-off line.

While I was wishing so hard for a Volvo, I figured that I might as well daydream about what else I don't have, can't have, and never will get. "So go for it," I told myself. "At least you can have happiness in your dreams." Happiness for me was the Volvo SUV. "Lord, the willow-green metallic one, please, and don't forget to add the forward-facing third-row seat for good measure. And, while You're at it, throw in the sunroof and the Bose stereo system with surround sound. I'll take TVs in the headrest, too. Houston is a big, traffic-congested place, and these long drives aren't going to entertain my activity-starved kids with just the scenery." I was certain that with this SUV, if we were ever to fall off a cliff or had an elephant come from out of nowhere to stand on my car, as the commercials used to suggest, my children would be safe.

God said no to the Volvo as well. At least at that time.

"Is that too much, God? Am I being selfish asking for luxury? Because I know Your Word, and Oprah says that You dream a bigger dream for me than I can dream for myself."

So, when it seemed that God wasn't listening, and I didn't get a seat in the "You get a car! You get a car! You get a car!" Oprah audience, I changed my request from a brand-new car to, "God? Can You at least give me a nice used car?"

It may sound foolish or selfish now, but in retrospect, my cries to God for anything was a reflection of where I was in my life. As the saying goes, "Hurt people, hurt people." So, the truth is that hungry people eat anything. When you're hungry, you will ask for things that you really don't want. It's dangerous to go to the grocery store when you're hungry. You're in this place where all the opportunity exists to produce anything that will fulfill your desire and curb your appetite. Quickly. Just like wealth gained hastily will dwindle (Proverbs 13:11) so too is food to the belly that has no sustenance. It's simple to say, "I want cookies. I want cake, and don't forget the crackers." In the grocery store, I start thinking of all of the things I'm not supposed to have. I start thinking about when I'm home later on and the snacks I'll need for watching television, which leads to seventeen bags of Skinny Pop popcorn because I'm hungry in a place of opportunity.

Filled people, on the other hand, aren't so easily enticed by things that aren't on their menu or in the plan. A satiated individual who has had their fill at a meal will not eagerly indulge in more food. When you are hungry, you can't concentrate on learning because you are thinking about how hungry you are. When you're fed, the focus can go to other needs that need to be met.

We do the same thing with God. When I wanted a car my request was specific, an intricately thought-out request. I knew the colors and options available. I had visited the dealership and even knew the particulars. When God didn't answer, I changed my request to something that really wouldn't satisfy nor supply my need.

Because what I really wanted was to be mobile. I wanted human interaction. I wanted to go from here to there, but my request wasn't thoughtfully considered, yet I wanted God to thoughtfully consider it for me. I wished I could have that job, but the one I asked for didn't align with God's purpose or plan for me. Sometimes we are thinking that God never answers any of our requests when, in fact, he's been paying attention to how we walked through the grocery store of life hungry.

Sometimes God had told us "No," but oftentimes I put things on my grocery list of requests that really weren't what I really wanted or needed. God saw my grocery lists in my prayers, but He also knew what I had stored in the refrigerator of my life. He knew what was packed in the freezer that I could pull out. He knew what could be thawed and cooked up tonight. We had things tucked away in the back, skill sets we hadn't developed. I didn't have to ask God to do a new thing when he'd already done the main thing. He already purchased the produce. We have to take time to pull it out of ourselves.

While canned goods and produce all have expiration dates, prayers to God never expire. Our prayers have a long shelf life, and if we ever make the time to be still, we might discover that what we prayed for led to getting something we actually wanted or needed.

That Volvo I described? Eventually, I got exactly that—an XC90, the exact color and model—about ten years after I made that request. It didn't come when I wanted it. It came many years later. I got it when I could afford to buy it with cash, insure it properly, and keep up the regular maintenance.

Growing Up Theodalinda's Daughter

*"If they're not talking about you,
then you're not worth talking about"* ~ Linda Theriot

Theodalinda Graham Theriot was a giant to me. I realized later that, even at 5'11", she wasn't as tall as she seemed when I was growing up. She wore a size thirteen women's shoe. Her beautiful curly hair was always kept short and tapered because she didn't like long hair. Her hair was everything mine was not.

I used to be embarrassed by her laugh, which was very full and very loud. I don't know why I was embarrassed to have a mother so full of joy that her laughter carried. Maybe it was because we lived in a third-floor apartment above the playground. When my mom would get on the phone, she laughed at the most obnoxious volume. Everyone could hear her from the jungle gym. "Mignon's mom is on the phone again."

"Do you think I am ever going to grow up?" I asked her later. I was already an adult in my forties.

"Well, if I'm any indication, it's never going to happen." She burst into laughter because, even at seventy-five, she was a kid at heart.

She was known by her village for being an energetic, lively, and playful host, and, for as long as I can remember, Mom was the life of the party.

What people liked most about our Louisiana kitchen was my mom's Midwestern flare. Every bit of her Topeka, Kansas, upbringing was celebrated in her NOLA kitchen, so meals with my mom were unusual by the local standards. No gumbo or dirty rice was steeping in her pots. Instead, we had tacos, pot pies, and casseroles. Accompanying the spread would always be some creative dessert like lemonade pie, blueberry banana cheesecake, or ambrosia.

I don't think anything was much better or garnered as many memories as Friday night gatherings and haystacks at our house. Nearly every Friday night my mom and her friend group gathered to end the week. As Adventists, there's pretty much no revelry on that night because it's the Sabbath (Sabbath eve, as I like to say), but laughter and food would be plentiful. My mother was the queen of a quick meal gathered around a bed of tortilla chips or corn chips (or Doritos if she was being fancy), layered with beans, taco meat (occasionally), lettuce, tomatoes, cheese, salsa, sour cream, black olives, and more. We called them "Haystacks," a term I learned is an Adventist word for tostadas or taco salad. It was one of those meals that you assign each guest a portion of the ingredients, and *voila*, it's a party! Those meals were limited only by time, ingredients in the pantry, or budget. Her friends would trickle in, each with a piece of the meal to participate.

Like other conservative Protestant religions, Seventh-day Adventists have a way about them, and my mother fit that mold very well. They'll bring you over to their house after church, never having seen you before, but by the end of the day, you belong to their tribe. That was my mother. Her hospitality was as big as she was tall. If no dinner was to be had at her house, you could find your way over to the one she was invited to.

Her generous and welcoming spirit probably came from her mother. Although my brother and I never knew her (she passed before we were born), my mom's stories about her were legendary. On Mondays, for instance, my grandmother would fill plates of food from her family dinner table for my grandfather to take lunches to the men at work who might not otherwise have a nice meal to eat. "Be sure to bring back my good china," Grandma would scold because Grandpa had a habit of leaving some of her plates and silverware behind. Mom would always smile when she told that story.

My mother would meet and marry a military man who would take her home to New Orleans to make a life. Linda, as my mom is known, belonged in the South. They loved her there. By "they," I mean everybody. I never heard a hateful word cast in my mother's direction. She worked the same primary job in communications at MetLife insurance company most of my life, and once we settled in a church, she was there to stay. She always held an office within the church as a servant, tithing her money and her time.

For as long as I can remember, my mom was enrolled in school. Though she only had a high school education for most of my life, one would be hard-pressed to know it by the way she distinctly and correctly pronounced words, spoke from an extensive vocabulary, and offered precise, thoughtful explanations. She was one to be admired and respected for the way she considered and treated others and her veracious work ethic. She graduated from college in 2016 with an associate's degree, exactly fifty years after her high school graduation in May 1966. She did it one class at a time. We celebrated with all the children and grandchildren as she walked up the steps and across the stage. They had to pause graduation because we were crunk. At age sixty-eight, she was by far the oldest person in her graduating class. We were so proud of her that we were literally screaming.

She was creative in the kitchen—and by creative, I mostly mean messy. When she prepared a meal, she dirtied every pot, pan, and dish in the kitchen. She expected her guests to eat and thoroughly enjoy the food using every fork, plate, and cup in the cupboard and never dare to lift a finger to clean, pack, or put anything away at the end. That was her hospitality.

I hated it, mostly because I had to clean it all up. It would take me hours upon hours to attack the piles of dishes that spanned every empty countertop and covered the stove. I think I've cried the most tears I can remember at the never-ending sink full of suds I have busted in my lifetime. I never understood why Dawn dishwashing liquid couldn't manage to get more than grease out of my way.

My brother Lamont's job? Take out the trash. So unfair! I think it was in my mom's kitchen that my fight for fairness, equity, and freedom ultimately began. It also was where I would begin the journey to who I was going to become.

The kitchen, the bane of my existence for years, boasted an uninspiring palette of inconspicuous browns. The cabinets were wood stained a mahogany brown. The tan Formica butcher block-style countertops gave contrast to the cabinets below. The variegated brown vinyl floors had a Mediterranean or even a Spanish-themed feel. The eating nook adjacent to the kitchen opened access to the rest of the living space, separated only by a wall with a cut-out serving window.

On that wall was our primary house telephone. The beige twenty-five-foot coiled phone cord gave Mom the freedom to be mobile while she cooked in stockinged feet and the A-line dress she'd worn to work that day.

Although you would never know it from her hospitality, she hated cooking.

As much as she entertained, you would think she enjoyed it. Definitely not so. Cooking was a chore for her. So, to pass the time, I think she drowned herself in church gossip, catching up with her sister about coupons, and who shot John, or checking on my grandmother, whom she loved dearly.

My mom's mother passed from this life and entered forever sleep when my mom was twenty-one years old. So, Mom made herself a family of elders and kin from my father's family and from the friends she made in church. My aunts are mostly her sister-friends; my cousins are the endless adoptees my mother collected from Sabbath dinners over the years, people who passed through town or were in the places we've lived.

Though we never met our maternal grandmother, we've had a host of surrogate grandparents. When she heard it takes a village, my mother gathered a town. Such an overachiever. Though her natural family was small, our surrogate one spread from sea to shining sea. Since unlimited long-distance calling would not come into being until years later, juggling the family tree was a task. She managed handsomely somehow on a shoestring, three-job budget, which consisted of her main full-time gig and two side gigs she managed at any given point. At one point, she worked as a cashier at Jim Dandy, a fried-chicken restaurant. They would give her chicken to bring home, but because she was a vegetarian, she didn't eat it. She did eat the salads she brought home, though. To this day, the one I watch her make the most is one she concocted from the same ingredients she could use from the Jim Dandy restaurant to make a meal.

She took on extra work at MetLife, even as she was succeeding in the full-time position she held there, processing claims at home in the evenings to supplement her pay. She was trying to make ends meet for her family. Looking back, she did it so well, my brother and I never even knew we were poor.

And we were not, at least not in a true sense. Her bank account often teetered on the brink of overdraft, but we were rich in so many other ways. And we were inventive with being frugal. We saved on electricity in minute and inventive ways. Washing dishes by hand was one of them, even though we had an electric dishwasher. Ours was used mainly to hide dishes I wasn't ready to put away, and my mom seemed to be fine with me drying the dishes there. Our home was equipped with a central air and heat system that could only be touched by our mom. It mostly could only be used at night, when the sweltering heat of New Orleans was too much. During the summer, both the blinds and the curtains were kept closed. We could never enjoy the light of the sun inside, not because she was an undercover vampire or anything; opening them meant allowing the cool to escape and the sun's heat to infiltrate. We lived under the cool of a ceiling fan by day in summer, and winter nights were warmed by the fire of a kerosene heater placed strategically in the family hall where all three bedrooms could get cozy under mountains of quilts and blankets.

She was an expert saver indeed, and with those savings, she managed to give us many of the luxuries that made our lives appear to be rich to those looking on. Because she lived like no one else, we got to have experiences that colored our lifestyle.

Mom always took us on an annual vacation, usually to a family member's house, so that we could keep up with our heritage. But here and there we had a sprinkling of trips to places such as Lookout Mountain in Tennessee, the Red Rocks of Colorado, Disneyland, and the beaches of California. I remember jumping into the Pacific Ocean wearing a two-tone avocado green bathing suit we had gotten from a thrift store. We saw a show in Branson, Missouri, and went to Bedrock City, Arizona and saw the Flintstones. I just knew that Pebbles and Bam-Bam were really playing back there. We skied in the Rockies as children, camped, and rode horseback. We went to the Grand Canyon and took a drive down the Las Vegas strip.

In my Southern Black girl experience, if nothing else screamed "rich kid," our travel adventures most certainly did. My mother made sacrifices to help us be well rounded, taking us places she should never have been able to afford.

I believe it was our mother's open-handed approach to mothering that made it easy for us to express ourselves freely. For instance, Lamont always felt he should ask for whatever he wanted, believing that she could just write a check to obtain it. He had no true understanding of the truth—we were living paycheck to paycheck and real, green dollars were needed to back up the checks written from her bank book. It was that same "tell me how you really feel" attitude that gave me the gall to say, "Mom, I hate doing these dishes. How about you and I make a deal?" Knowing her affinity for cooking, I had the clever idea that I would offer to cook all of the weekly meals for the household with one small catch. She would wash all the dishes.

"You've got a deal," she quickly agreed.

Now, all I had to do was figure out cooking.

I went to the source of all my favorite food experiences, my grandmother, my father's adoptive mother. My mom budgeted everything. So even talking long distance to Grandma to get this accomplished would have to be metered. Mom said we could allot five minutes for the call. (Remember, this was in the days when we paid for long-distance telephone calls by the minute.) I wasn't sure what I could learn that fast, but I was willing to take it.

Years later, I would again consult my grandmother when I wanted to learn how to make my first successful cake. And because I had spent so much time learning from her over the phone, and learning it quickly, I was able to perfect her strawberry cake and my confidence in the kitchen when it was time to create a recipe I could build a legacy on.

Down on the Bayou

"A smile is your greatest social asset."
~ Zig Ziegler

In many ways I could rightly claim that my soul was born on the bayou. As a teen, I learned to drive myself there, traveling the stretch of Highway 90 so I could spend weekends with my cousins Michael and Wendy. They were the closest family members my age within hundreds of miles and helped make up the perfect space where a blooming teenage girl like me could expand her horizons. While I was visiting, my older cousin Tam and my father's baby sister, Michelle, who we called Leisa, would occasionally sneak me off to the skating rink with them.

"Play another slow jam, this time make it sweet." I loved Midnight Star's "Slow Jam" hit because Tam did, and I still do. The way she swayed her head from side to side, smacking her lips between stanzas made me want to appreciate that song as much as she did, along with another of their hits, "No Parking on the Dance Floor."

I loved the music I grew up on—Midnight Star, Freddie Jackson classics, and "Juicy Fruit" by Mtume, to name a few. My older cousins would be practicing the new dances in my grandmother's living room and try to entice me to join them, but I was so shy that I wouldn't dance in front of them. I tried it though. After they left the house and I was certain no one could see me, I'd try out the dance moves I'd seen them practice.

Cousin life for me was a thing of siblinghood and friendship. Chaundra, who is six months younger than me, was my first best friend. Anya and Tanya, my twin cousins, carried me along on dates when I was the only little girl cousin around. I got in trouble when my brother told on me because I had gone to the movies to see John Travolta in *Urban Cowboy,* and on the Sabbath at that. But of all the cousins, I saw something I wanted to possess in my beautiful cousin Tam. With everything I had in me, I wanted to be like her. Likely some of the joy I've become known for can be attributed to my experience of Tam. She was long-legged, blonde, and beautiful. Hers were full and ample lips she kept painted in a rouge red color. I found joy in just watching Tam be. She modeled who I wanted to be. Her! One thing I managed to literally photocopy in my mind was Tam's smile. When she smiled, she stretched her mouth from ear to ear with a joy that lit up the room. I stood in the mirror to practice just how I could manipulate my mouth and make a smile that would radiate joy. Literally hours of practice.

I didn't know then a truth that I know now—that smile would bring joy to others and add to my face value. Before then, people would ask me what I was always down about. My general "deep-in-thought" face could be easily interchanged with my "Why-are-you-talking-to-me?" face, my "Who-you-lookin'-at-with-a-face-like-that?" face, and my "blank-stare" face—all at the same time.. After practicing my smile, people began to ask me what I was so happy about and that has added not only face value but has been a bankable asset. Trying to emulate Tam's style, I learned to embrace my full lips, but that's all I managed to appreciate about myself. It would be a long time coming before I realized that, like Dorothy in *The Wizard of Oz*, I had what I desired all along.

The woman I called Grandma was not related by blood. But she was the woman who had raised my father since before he began formal schooling. My father went to live on the bayou with Morris "Sunny" Watson and Virginia "Aunt Jenny" Matthews-Watson when he was about four or five years old.

I've heard many variations of the family's history regarding the reasons why my dad went to the bayou to live with them. I've determined, having heard so many variations of the story, that the truth will be one of those parts in history that got buried with the people who lived it. (It's also the reason I am telling my story now, so that it doesn't die when I do.) Whatever the reason, Sunny and Jenny brought my dad home with them while other family members along the bayou picked up some of his siblings. When the time came for his real mother to collect her children again, my father didn't go with her. A cousin hid him in the chicken coop while they searched for him. And for the next several years my father remained there in Bayou Black, Louisiana, until he graduated from high school in 1965.

During what would be our last conversation with our dad before his untimely and sudden death in 2021, he did share one anecdote that connects us back to who we are and our family name, Theriot. After high school, Dad was heading back to the Bayou on military leave, getting off the bus in New Orleans, when someone recognized the name embroidered on his uniform. "I know your pedigree," the man said to my father, who was shocked and excited to meet someone familiar with the family name. My father had returned to using it upon entering the US Air Force. That someone turned out to be Joachim Woodridge, his brother-in-law, his older sister Yvonne's husband. My father followed him to my Aunt Ethel May's house, his eldest sister, where he was reunited with his family by a chance crossing at a bus terminal.

Here's what I know for certain about my dad. For one, he has two birth dates—August 6 and August 11. I believe that when he started school on the bayou, they were unsure of his actual birth date and simply gave him one. It wasn't until a copy of his birth certificate surfaced that we learned he wasn't even born in New Orleans, but rather in a grocery store on Bessie Kay, which is a street on the plantation where my grandparents lived.

His memory had begun to fade by the time I got a chance to ask my father questions about his early years, and it wasn't clear why recalling any of this made him so angry. So honestly, we may never know how he ended up living on the bayou, the child of a couple who had no children of their own at the time. I may never know the motivation behind the adoptive mother who loved her son's wife and daughter so much that she poured deeply into both of them and created for me the space to become who I am today. Without Grandma Jenny, there would be no foundation for my ability to cook in the kitchen with Southern girl slay, no understanding for thickening roux, and baking the award-winning cakes that would bring me notoriety all around the world.

I spent a lot of time visiting Grandma on the bayou, and every now and then she would visit us in New Orleans. Our house wasn't the most comfortable place for my grandmother, so she didn't visit often. She was most comfortable maintaining her responsibilities at home, knowing the carryings-on of her relatives who stopped by her house daily for general gossip, catch-up sessions, or a delicious meal. Those most valued times are what I remember most regarding the things my grandmother taught me—how to hold the bean pod just right to snap the ends off quickly, the value of not letting people know how you really feel. Most of all, I treasured that she understood the decisions I was making, even though they weren't always the best.

At home, I complained a lot about food, and I always wanted something that wasn't being offered, but the one place I could always expect to get something I really wanted to eat was at Grandma's house. Even though we ate in a way that was somewhat foreign to my grandmother, she did her best to accommodate us. Much of the time we were vegetarians and other times we were not. Although my mother teetered back and forth, we never ate pork and followed a strict guideline regarding what seafood was safe to eat—all things that were foreign to my grandmother's way of cooking. My absolute favorite meal was pot roast with gravy over rice, accompanied by green peas swimming in butter. That would be my last meal if I were on death row. My lips smack thinking about it; I can almost taste it now. My grandmother would stuff the roast with whole pieces of fresh garlic and sear it in butter before retiring it to the oven for most of the day. Her gravy was a thick roux acquired from pouring boiling water in the burnings of what was left from searing the roast. That delicious concoction poured over rice was like liquid gold to me.

Grandma was a robust woman, with a bosom that beckoned you to come and rest a while. Her hands seemed stuffed to capacity, so that her skin sort of shined. These were hands that had washed her weight and mine in dishes and laundry. Maybe they were hands that bore signs of aging even in her youth.

She had a quiet joy about her and was an expert at multitasking. She loved to cook and would even spend her money to cook for other people. She was always cooking. Always! When taking a break from cooking, Grandma would sit down to watch her favorite soap operas, specifically *General Hospital* and *The Young and the Restless*. Whether taking a break to enjoy television, or actively holding a conversation with family members, my grandma could fall asleep at any moment. A deep, satisfying sleep that called the hogs home with loud snoring. She worked so hard that I imagine her taking time to be tired would have to come much later. No matter how soundly she slept in front of that television, we dared not turn it off. Though we will never know how she did it, you could never actually "catch" my grandmother sleeping. And snoring was not an indication of slumber. She knew what was happening around her at all times, and never missed a beat in the conversation nor the scene on the soap opera.

Once, my brother walked by her napping comfortably on the sofa and turned the television off.

"Boy, what you do that for?"

"Grandma, you were sleeping," he replied.

In her rebuke, she would ramble off the very scene and conversation that was happening before my brother had hit the switch. She offered proof that she could sleep and watch television at the same time.

Grandma loved going to church and was there every Sunday. She was poor and she struggled for everything, but she was faithful to pay her tithes and worried over her offerings even on her deathbed. All that she had she would give away for those she loved. She never said anything bad about anybody. She was a homebody who didn't expect much. But she loved to go shopping, especially for shoes. Even though she had very little money, she had plenty of shoes, whether they were hand-me-downs or dime-store finds.

"Shoe Town…that's my sto'," she would say.

Grandma was meticulous about her appearance. Her hair was always done, usually dyed plum or some eccentric red color, with a closely tapered layered cut.

If you gave her five dollars, she offered fifty dollars' worth of gratitude in return.

Everybody loved her. She belonged to everybody, but somehow, I believed she belonged mostly to me.

On the Road with Theodalinda

"It is not the destination where you end up but the mishaps and memories you create along the way!" ~ Penelope Riley

Our mom believed that education didn't always mean sitting in a classroom, behind a desk, or with a traditional teacher. She believed in taking us out of school to travel. We would take our homework and finish it on the road. We played a lot of games in the car and listened to country music on the radio. My mom loved country music and Christianity. Those were her two speeds.

While we occasionally had the privilege to ride on planes, our summer vacations were mostly road trips that included stops where we had a free place to stay, like a relative or friend's house. But getting to those vacations, or should I say back from those vacations, was the proving ground for her faith. It was the stuff that makes me believe in miracles because I've experienced them firsthand.

On one particular trip, I remember Mom buying bread, peanut butter, and jelly for the journey. I wanted bologna. "You've got peanut butter and jelly, Mignon," was her unenthused response.

She had overindulged us a little too much and didn't have enough cash for the gas we would need to get home. In those days, gas stations had full-service options, and she had to be strategic and chose self-serve lanes only to avoid having to tip the attendant for pumping gas and washing windows, something we children were capable of doing. Gas companies would offer rebates to patrons who used cash to purchase their gas. So, with each stop, my mom collected rebates ranging from twenty-five cents to seventy-five cents, which she would add to her coin purse after each fill-up.

At the last stop, she gathered all her rebates to fill the car but fell short of the full tank needed to complete the trip. Lamont and I immediately went into prayer mode, offering our immature petitions, "Oh, God, help us, please." My brother roared with intention as he petitioned God to get us home. I believe somewhere in that I learned that God has a heart for the prayers of children. They worked. Not only did we make it home, but she also drove on that gas for the rest of that week until payday on Friday.

Mom was very open about her faith, and she was quite transparent in sharing her challenging moments with us. When my mom was victorious, she praised the Lord in front of us. When times were lean, if she was afraid or worried, she talked about those things with us as well. She didn't sugarcoat anything, but she still managed to protect our childhood innocence. I remain grateful to God that my mom lived a life in front of her children that would preach. She taught us life lessons as she learned them from the school of hard knocks, and that is where I can pinpoint the first evidence I gathered that God would show up for me if I positioned myself to see Him. I learned firsthand from my mother's example of leadership that God would show Himself stronger the more I accepted my own weakness.

An Angel Named Fishburn

"Bring the whole tithe into the storehouse.... Test me in this,"
says the Lord Almighty...." (Malachi 3:10, NIV)

Perhaps the most impactful memory of my mother's leadership and depth of faith dates back to Denver 1979. Mom had rented a two-bedroom, red-brick ranch fourplex. We had one bathroom in the hall between the two small bedrooms where the kids slept. The wood floors were stained a honey color, worn darker from our foot traffic. One night I saw what looked like a bear standing in the doorway looking in on us. It moved, better yet glided through the hall. I hadn't yet decided if it was a ghost when it stopped to look directly at me. I screamed and covered up my head before it spoke to me.

"Mignon, what's wrong?" It was a soothing and familiar voice, but I was not comforted in that moment.

"I'm scared there's a bear." By now my heart was probably in my throat.

The voice came closer to comfort me. It turned out to be my mother's shadow that I saw in the door frame, and her who told me it would be okay. Ever since that day I have seen my mom as a giant.

Our kitchen, south of the family living room, had a Dutch door leading to the backyard, which was nothing more than a patchwork of dust, for no grass ever grew there. Mom always parked her car in one of the spots just off of the wooden back porch and climbed the two steps that I remember being worn for wear but not quite rickety. Her butterscotch gold Pontiac Grand Prix was a very popular car that felt like a sports car to me. The seats were a velvety gold fabric. My uncle, one of those church members I spoke about earlier, cosigned for my mom to get that car at a used car lot.

Besides these, I have only one other memory of that house, and it was an experience that forever changed my life. That was the day an angel named Fishburn showed up to bless our family.

Just off the small kitchen area of the home, which had been built sometime in the 1950s or 60s, was a steep, unfinished staircase that descended into the basement where my mom had her makeshift sanctuary. Her king-sized bed was posited in the middle of the floor, dominating in the dank, dark, spooky space, with only the water heater and washing machine to keep her company. A thin peach-colored quilt covered in large flowers decorated the top of her bed. Underneath the bedposts was a floor rug that a church member brought her from a hotel being remodeled. A single dim light added warmth to her space.

I remember the setup so vividly because I was terrified of the dark and even more afraid of being alone in it. One day, I was tasked with venturing down into Mom's scary abyss to fetch something she needed, guided only by the light of the open door above. Once I was too far to run back up and reach the door quickly, my brother slammed it, cutting off my light source. I may have peed my pants in panic, frantically fishing for the light cord in the middle of the room. Flailing my arms through the air, I was desperately searching to release the light bottled in that single bulb. Even after I found the light, it wasn't enough to settle my pounding heart. I clutched what I had come for and scurried up the stairs, trying my best not to fall through the gaping side of the scant basement stairs.

On the day before that life-changing Saturday, Mom had gotten paid and had used her entire check to pay her bills. All she had left from her previous week of labor were the coins in her change purse for catching the bus to work during the coming week. We didn't have a car at that time, the telephone had been disconnected, and we were relatively new to Denver. The car she had previously was a lemon, even though she had purchased it new. Unable to keep up with repairs and car payments, she let the car go back to the dealer.

We were on our own. We had retired to Mom's chilly basement bedroom to snuggle underneath a pile of blankets and her warm embrace. The knock on our door compelled her to gather her statuesque frame and climb the steps slowly, while hoping the visitor would go away quickly. I went with her because I was afraid to stay in the basement alone. Brother Wilkerson, the leader of our Pathfinder Club from church, wanted to borrow some vinegar. He was a very tall, dark man with a faint grin adorned by a curled mustache. His distinguished salt and pepper hair did not offer a hint of his age. His shiny, brown skin was smooth and uncracked by time. He was the epitome of "black don't crack."

Adventist families are strict about working, buying, and selling on the Sabbath, so he couldn't simply go to the store and get some. Off to the kitchen, my mother pulled the bottle from her cupboards and told him to help himself to all of it. She wanted to get back to the nap we had just settled in for. Bounding back down the stairs, I was clicking close to her heels. There's no way I would lead the journey back down into the deep.

Soon after we were back in bed, we heard another knock. Again? Wrestling with the covers in a fit of disgust and aggravation, my mother made her way back to the front door for what seemed like a never-ending stretch of stairs and traversed the living-room floor.

That Saturday was also Valentine's Day. On the other side of the wooden door, through the half-moon shaped glass, my mother spied a lady she had met only once before. I had never seen her, nor have

I seen her since. The woman, Cora Mae Fishburn, was a friend of a friend from my mother's childhood in Kansas. She and the daughter who accompanied her now lived in Denver, just a few streets away. She was petite with brown skin, the color of sweet milk chocolate.

I don't remember her being overly happy or joyful. I think I have always paid attention to expressions. I was a very timid girl who could read whether people liked me, or so I thought. I stayed close to my mother as she invited them into our small living room. Just beyond the door, the woman took a seat on the piano bench, vowing not to stay for long.

"I tried to call you, but your phone is not working," Mrs. Fishburn said, settling herself on the bench where my mother played hymns for us. She loved that piano. My father had bought it for her on their first wedding anniversary. Ours was a musical family, and this was her instrument.

"I just wanted to come by and wish you a happy Valentine's Day," she said, reaching into her purse and handing a card to my mother. My mom stood from the sofa offering an uncertain smile. She was indeed grateful for everything she received, but never took too easily to people giving her gifts, especially from people she didn't know well.

"Oh, you didn't have to give me a card," Mom said as she accepted the token of kindness. Sitting back on the couch, my mother started opening the envelope when Mrs. Fishburne interrupted. "Why don't you just wait until after we leave? Besides, it's just a card, nothing special," she assured my mom.

My impatient mother somehow mustered the discipline to let that card burn a hole in her lap for the remainder of the visit, which seemed like an eternity but probably was no more than five minutes.

As mother and daughter drove away, Mom nervously held the card as Lamont and I anxiously drew near to get a closer look. She ripped open the envelope, curious as to what could be inside. Why didn't she think it was just a card as her kind new friend had indicated?

Mom's instincts were right. Out of the card fell a $50 bill and a check for $250. We moved in closer to get a better look. Stunned is an apt description of my mother at that moment. Frozen and stiff. Michelle, my sister-aunt, was in the kitchen. Since my mom likes to prank, Michelle offered a sarcastic "Uh-uh," in disbelief. Michelle was my mother's youngest sister whom she had raised since age five when their mother died. Although Michelle is my aunt, we grew up like sisters since she's only ten years older than me. She had recently moved back to New Orleans after divorcing her husband, and I was glad to have my big sister back. She wore the same size clothing that I did, and with so many of my closest girlfriends growing up with a gang of sisters, I wanted Michelle to be mine. I loved her like that anyway, not like an auntie. You get to share things with sisters, like secrets and sneakers and advice.

With no phone to call and say thank you, and no car to go by her house, Mom waited for Monday to come so she could call Mrs. Fishburn from work and express her gratitude.

"I'm so happy that you gave me this card with this money in it, but I don't know why you did it," Mom said. "I will pay you back."

Mom was newly on her own after leaving our father in New Orleans, and coming to Denver was sucking up every extra dime she had saved. Aside from her piano, the living room furniture must have been made up of discards her brother Jimmy gave her.

"You will not be paying me back. You're not going to make me lose my blessing," Mrs. Fishburne retorted, describing how God had led her there to bless us. "Your phone was off, and I knew you had those children. God told me to go to you."

That night we feasted on our dinner from Pizza Hut.

Earlier that day in church, my mother had a little talk with Jesus as the offering plate was passing by. Clutching her tithe in her purse, she knew she had one chance to make a good decision. Moving the family to Denver to escape her abusive marriage to our father took all that she had saved. She had to drive a U-Haul truck hundreds of miles to the Midwest where she could rely on the support of her siblings nearby. She didn't have much, and everything depended on budgeting what she did have, including that tithe money that she felt the urging in her spirit to give up to God. Without that money, she would have nothing until Friday, except those coins in her change purse.

"That's not your money," she heard God say, recalling the story when years later we asked why she was such a faithful tither. Taking a deep inhale, followed by a sigh, she released the money into the velvet-lining of the shiny gold offering plate, after which the suited ushers marched back to the altar to offer the church members' monetary sacrifices back to the Lord.

"A conscious decision had been made, and I didn't know what I would do," she recalled years later.

That's the faith of my mother, to believe whatever God says to her. I wouldn't say that she has unwavering obedience. No. She's definitely going to test the waters and be sure that God indeed was talking to her. He was. She may not have known what God's plan would be for the coming week, but she knew what she would do that day.

The first indicator of God's plan came as she crossed the church parking lot with us kids in tow, making our way to catch the bus that soon would be barreling down the road. She hoped aloud that we hadn't missed it. Turns out it wouldn't matter, not that day. As we were making our way across the lot, Aunt Ola pulled up in the family van she called the Blue Goose and offered us a ride home. Filing into that big blue van was always an adventure. Aunt Ola had a jubilant spirit and chuckled with a hearty joyful laughter. To me, she looked a lot like my mom, and Oprah Winfrey sometimes. She dropped us off and promised to come back on Monday to take us to school for the rest of the week. Meanwhile, Mom had to muster the fifty cents she would need to get to and from work Monday. She had no idea in the moment, but she wouldn't need to concern herself with that. God had a blessing with her name on it.

That three hundred dollars from Mrs. Fishburn was a lot of money for a single mom to accept from a near stranger, especially with no prospect of how she could ever pay it back. In fact, any attempt at payback would be frowned upon, as repayment might block the giver's blessings. That is the stuff that Lifetime and Hallmark movies are made of. That was a lot of money in those days. Probably all, or maybe even more than our mother was accustomed to receiving after a hard week of work.

I never forgot that lady, nor could I ever forget the day that she came on Valentine's Day to show love to a woman and her children who appeared to be lacking a little of that one thing. Love. The day was clear and crisp, the sky sprinkled with cottony clouds, and an impression would be forever made in the mind of a five-year-old girl, from that one encounter on a Sabbath day. It was there my siblings and I coined the phrase "a Mrs. Fishburn moment," to signify the little miracles that happen in life, whether you experience them firsthand or you extend the hand that offers it. I knew what I really wanted to be when I grew up. I wanted to be a miracle, to be a blessing, instead of looking for one.

Who You With?

There is nothing better than a cake, but more cake."
~ Harry S. Truman

Throughout most of my childhood, it seemed like the final school bell of the summer would barely have rung before Lamont and I were packed in a car or booked on a flight back to New Orleans to spend summers with our dad.

With:

"a preposition, accompanied by (another person or thing)."

I hardly ever remember being "with" my dad. Alvin Theriot was a hard-working nine-to-five man, always off from work and back out again to play at the nightclub scene or build someone else's house. Besides the occasional pass through the living room on his way up the stairs to his room, or him bounding down the stairs after having come home to change before heading back out the door, I think most of my memories with him involve opening his wallet. I barely ever remember him hanging around to "visit." The person we spent time with was Altamease.

Although they were divorced, our parental tribe was made up of amicable co-parents, all three of them. My mom, my dad, and Altamease, the only woman I had ever known to be with my father, besides my mother, and who later married my dad. He provided for us. He was present, as much as men in those days believed was their responsibility to be. By present I mean, we knew our dad by name and his character. He was ours, he just wasn't ever there for anything fun.

All summer long, I also played with the little girl across the hall, an only child of two parents who clearly and demonstrably loved her. Dee Dee was happy, and when she smiled her cheeks turned the shade of pink roses. After school, she excitedly ripped off her uniform skirt to climb the steep mountain of stairs that led to their apartment door across from ours. We could play as soon as I had practiced my flute and she had finished her homework. I appreciated her so much, and of all the children I had encountered at school, nobody willed me to play as much as Dee Dee did. We played together gleefully, mostly on the playground or in her upstairs room, until her mother said it was time for me to go home. I don't know why but she rarely came to our house, except on my birthday for cake and ice cream.

I never remember having cake at my mom's house (except the cheesecake sometimes served for Sabbath, which isn't the same). My love for white cake with pineapple filling comes from summers at Dad's with Altamease.

Altamease loved cake, and thought everybody should have one to celebrate. Every July 4, along with a gift-wrapped box on my bed when I woke up, a sugary, snowy-white birthday cake from Mackenzie's bakery would appear at the house. It would be dressed in drapes of yellow or orange swags and buttercream flowers. Sandwiched in between the layers was a bright yellow pineapple glaze that cut some of the sweetness. It always left a pasty aftertaste in my mouth but never enough to stop me from craving it.

I loved my birthday because we had cake for days. I loved my brother's birthday, too, which was only sixteen days after mine, so we got more cake. I always wanted the corner slice, if we were lucky enough to have a square cake, or a slice with a decorative rose to get the extra icing. When nobody was looking, I would draw my finger across the cardboard paper base and scrape up whatever icing had hardened there overnight.

Altamease's love for cake and the flavor she loved best was not passed down to me through birth, but rather through the joy of celebration. Those birthdays were slices of life etched into my memory. For me, the joy of eating cake is to be taken back to a time or place when someone genuinely saw and celebrated me.

I believe that to revere food as good is based on the experience and the memories you had with that food. That experience of cake with her and with my grandmother, too, were the foundation upon which I built an adoration for cake and an award-winning cupcake brand. Altamease saw and celebrated me. We didn't share DNA but we do share a love for pineapple-filled white cake. She may not be my birth mother, but she did birth within me the love for birthday cake, and that bonded us through many joyful times with something that brought us mutual enjoyment.

Be Careful What You Speak

Growing up, I always wanted my parents to get back together. Don't all children want that? Kids don't understand the often complicated dynamics of adult relationships. Children just want what they want—and often that's a mom and dad under the same roof.

My dad was very handsome. He was a clean-cut man, who always dressed well. He had black hair, and he often sported a beard. He was light-skinned, but his skin tone was browned by the sun from many years of working outside. He was somewhat slim, but he was always trying to gain weight. I was very proud to look at him as my father, but most of all, his generosity was an inspiration. My father believed in quality and was vocal about that. He had a collection of Rolex watches, suits that were tailored in other countries, and a classic Corvette that he cherished. If you admired something he had, one of his watches, for example, he might take it off and give it to you. He had an affection for pastors. If he learned about one who never had a tailored or custom suit, he might arrange for one at his own expense.

I don't remember him ever being in the same household with us and our mother, except for the one time he came to Denver to visit at Christmas. I had gotten a wooden dollhouse that year. It looked like a mansion made of Popsicle sticks. I loved it because he was there with us, and he put it together for me. I thought it meant that he was moving in with us again. I remember asking if he could, but he snapped at me. He disappeared behind the bedroom door, and the next morning, he was gone. That was it. My only fulfillment of my daddy being there for me when I wanted him.

The following summer we were again sent to New Orleans to spend time with our dad. Rubbing the crud from my sleepy eyes, I crawled into his oversized, shiny leather chair. It was burgundy and swallowed me up in a way that made me feel safe. "Good morning," I heard a lady's voice say from the kitchen. I slid deeper into the chair, ignoring the stranger who was not my mother.

My scolding came harshly, but that's about all my father would do. He barked. Loudly. That was enough to make me cry. No, sob. I don't recall affectionate embraces or gentle prodding from my father. Everything was rough. It intimidated me. My father had a strange way of showing affection. Maybe it wasn't his fault. You parent the way you were parented, they say.

My parents were total opposites. My mother was effortlessly nurturing and coddling. My dad was abrupt, sharp, and always on edge. To me that was mean. I felt as if he didn't even like me very much. Only me. If my dad didn't love me, then I was not lovable, and that became my narrative.

My dad would say nice things about his other children, but I never remember him saying anything nice about me. "Mignon, girl, you are getting fat like your mom." I heard that a lot. When we would go shopping for clothes, he would shower my brother with shoes, clothes, accessories, and other things. When it came to me, he would say, "Hurry up and pick something. That's too much money. Put that back. I'm not spending money on that."

So, I felt like I always had to pay for what was supposed to be rightfully mine. I wanted a job, my own money, and someone to be thrilled at the thought of buying me nice things.

He married Altamease when I was about seventeen years old, but she had been a strong presence in my life since I was age five. When we stayed with them in the summer, by the dawn of the first August sunrise, I was ready to go home to my mother.

My relationship with my father was complex, but it never stopped me from wishing for more, and it never stopped us from saying we wanted to be back there when we didn't get our way at Mom's house. Words like "I hate it here," or "I want to live with my daddy" are hard to swallow back when your mother makes you eat those words for an entire school year—breakfast, lunch, and dinner. That's exactly what happened the summer before I entered the fourth grade. She didn't pick us up at the end of the summer.

"If your dad is so great, you can stay with your dad." She meant it. We stayed with my dad in New Orleans and started school.

I'll always remember that first day at Schaumburg Elementary in Mrs. E. Raser's class. I thought her name sounded out, "Mrs. Eraser," was funny. She was a frail-looking, older white lady with short hair that was white with slivers of gray. She looked over glasses and pursed her lips at the children. When roll call came on the first day, the cadence in the name calling slowed to an ever-so-brief pause as she scanned her mind for how she would pronounce my name. Whatever she conjured up could not have been any person's real name.

"MIG-NON Tha-riot, she said, her lack of exposure showing.

I pushed my hand into the air that felt like peanut butter, not wanting to answer to such ridiculousness. It will always aggravate me that grown people do not take the time to know my name. I am flabbergasted to this day that people called me "Mig-Non."

We had a Spanish teacher who made matters worse. He could pronounce my first name but couldn't make sense of my last name. I liked him though. He smiled when he said, "No" when you got the answers wrong; he would encourage his students to keep trying until they got it right.

What I loved most about this fourth-grade class was also the thing I equally hated. There were Black girls who looked like me, who liked things I liked, who had parents they didn't know, and had dads that lived in other cities. I fit in with those kids, and at recess, I got my equal share of being it, and tagged in for the game because it was a game that everybody was worthy of playing.

Lunchtime was the part I hated, mostly because I was intimidated by the sixth graders there. I had never been to a school so big, but I had Tonya, a round-faced, caramel-colored girl with sandy hair like mine, a giant smile, and a laugh that was contagious. She sat next to me in class and at lunch. We looked so much alike that we told people we were cousins.

This was my first time going to school without my brother (who was in middle school), catching a school bus, and having to get up on my own in time for school. Most days it was pretty easy to get to the bus on time, barring those days I wet the bed. No one wants to wake up to cold wet legs. I would pray so hard hoping dear God in heaven would hear me, so I wouldn't have to wake up and try to shove the sheets in a hamper, and grab new ones to remake the bed, which was complicated by the fact it was in the corner of the room. Then I would have to manage to get another bath in before the school bus came.

Altamease and my dad were gone to work by the time the school bus came, but she would wake us up in the morning to FM98, an R&B radio station in New Orleans. Popular music was always playing throughout the house. It was a very musical household.

That year I got introduced to my flute and played in the school band. I could have my dad's undivided attention when I practiced. When the band director said I had the best form and would be a natural if I practiced, that made my father proud. He wasted no time in getting me a Bundy flute. I wanted the other brand with the sleeker case, but I knew not to complain. At least he wasn't making me play that dreadful clarinet. Every day, thirty minutes were set aside for

practice. I mostly
the basics but pai(
school band flute

I called my m
tantrums on the fl(
I moved mostly in
what I was given
had an awful swe(
was that I didn't
one day, I broke
things trying to u
by the case. I cou
microwaved syru|
she came home. :
was terrified of h(
I didn't want to b
but back then, tha

Near Christm
love interest who
her new car, whic
was excited to tak
equally excited fc

I tried to con
outside the car. l
leaving. I always
that, but I wasn't
of a three-story b(
steps and through
touching the door
didn't answer. I k
eased the door op

I saw him lyin
He was laying on
yellow flowers. T:

I said, "Dad, di
"All right."

I had crept ovel
He was. "I love you
response. None can

"I love you, Dac
silence that filled th
did. He spoke.

"Mignon, how
replied after a long

I walked away l

I tucked my he
back like a sad pup
had said that. He ne
in my direction. He
underwear type, but

I had seen them l
and bare-chested. I (
fact a summer day. (
His thick black bea
stairs, tying the whit
I remember it so vi
do his dirty work.

"Go ask Dad if
shoving me toward

"Why do I have

"He'll say yes t(

"Uh, Da-Dad, (
nervously with one
quickly out of his w

d you hear me say I'm leaving?

to the side of the bed to see if he was awake.
," I said waiting for him to return an obligatory
e.

d. Did you hear me?" I repeated. I waited for the
e space to ease some of its grip on me. It never

can I love you when I don't love myself?" he
pause.

believing that my dad didn't love me.

d in my sleeve and carried that away, looking
py to be sure he really didn't just say that. He
ver lifted his head from the pillow nor turned it
laid there in his baby-blue boxer shorts. Not the
his actual boxing shorts.

before. He was bounding down the steps barefoot
can't remember if it was a Saturday, but it was in
Our dad had an athletic build with little body fat.
rd always glistened. He was coming down the
e strings that dangled from his black waistband.
vidly because my brother had pushed me up to

he will take us to McDonald's!" Lamont said,
the stairs as Dad was preparing to come down.

to do it?"

you," Lamont reassured me.

can you take us to McDonald's?" I stuttered
foot stepping down from the steps backing
ay.

"We are going to have McDonald's right in that kitchen," he barked, never slowing his momentum, like a boulder picking up speed.

"Pancakes?" I brightened up.

"You're gonna have grits and eggs in this kitchen, Mignon," he commanded.

They don't make grits at McDonald's. I pouted, looking over at my brother, who was snickering at me.

"Lamont wanted it, too!" I pointed with a whining slur.

He ignored me, went into the kitchen, and made grits and eggs.

I hated grits, and I think I equally hated eggs. I did not belong there, and nobody cared about that.

I watched as my brother mixed his into one complimentary dish. I stared at mine. Staring only made the grits hard and more difficult to eat.

"Mix them!" my brother offered. "It tastes good this way."

I mixed them. They didn't taste good this way. Now the eggs, which were palatable on their own, were so covered in grits that I couldn't eat those either.

My dad took up residence on the brown plaid sofa with the dark-chocolate leather straps and propped his bare feet across the arm.

"I hate grits," I said, pouting.

"You shouldn't have mixed them," my brother teased.

"You told me to do it." I slumped into my chair as my brother was getting up from the table.

I stood up from the table thinking I would follow him.

Without even turning his head, which was propped by his left hand, Dad, who was watching the television that had been perched on top of the floor model, yelled, "Sit down and eat that food."

So, I sat and sat. More accurately, I gagged and sat until my dad got up and forgot about me. When he disappeared upstairs, I slithered from my seat, scraped the rest into the trash, and tucked it under the other trash that was already in there. I ran over for one last glance up the shaded steps toward the third-floor bedroom where my father had disappeared, to see if he was truly gone. He was. And then it was my turn to disappear.

I hate grits. I hate grits. I hate grits. I don't care if you put sugar on them. I don't care if you salt them or drown them in butter. I don't care about the debate over how they should be eaten. All I know is that I don't want them. Don't say it's because I have never had yours. I don't care! I do not want them here or there. I do not want them anywhere! Why is it that nobody catered to me? Ever! Why didn't anybody care about what Mignon wanted?

That question haunted my childhood. I have spent my life replaying words my father said to me when I was nine years old. I wondered if my siblings had known how it felt to hear that and not know what you'd done to deserve it. I was angry with him. I had questions for him and for God that I wanted answered. "When is he going to acknowledge me? When is he going to show up for me? When is he going to choose me? When is it going to be my turn?"

I felt that if my dad didn't love me, I was unlovable. That started feeding into my spirit. The devil will trick you into believing negative messages about yourself to get you off your calling. I had that feeling of not ever being good enough or wanted or chosen.

Like many men of his generation, my dad was a man who needed to be working. He defined his manhood and fatherhood by his capacity to work and provide for his family. That's also how he demonstrated his love. When Dad came to Nashville to stay with my family after Hurricane Katrina and help us with renovating our house, he would get up early every morning and start working on the house with my husband, François. They got so much done together. My dad gets a lot of credit for helping to get our house in order before I opened the bakery. I'm really grateful for those days for many reasons. I was grateful for the work being done on our house, but more than that, I was grateful for the time he spent with us because that's when I really got to know my father. It was time for me to really know him without the stressors of life weighing him down. He went back to New Orleans weeks later, but after Katrina he was never really the same. I think Katrina took our dad from us, the way that we knew him.

Along with all of her devastation, Hurricane Katrina brought with her a new normal that we never really got used to. When my sister moved back home to immerse her daughter into the music program, she didn't know it would come with a front-row seat to the drama that had become her parents' lives. She got a front row seat to arguments no child wants to see her parents having. Phone calls became graphic as she described the scene from which she wanted a reprieve. Desperate to make sense of what should have been their golden years and a growing intolerance to watch the saga that was becoming their lives, my siblings and I decided to hatch a plan to diffuse his bad behavior toward Altamease. For weeks we planned by phone to come together and present a united front.

We gathered for that "intervention" in January 2021. It was the last time we would all be together. We journeyed down to New Orleans to discuss a solution and to announce to our father the demands we were setting forth. He was getting help. On the day of our planned coup, we looked to our brother to lead the way. What he led was a walk down memory lane and a barrage of photos ensued after. All we did was laugh and enjoy each other's company.

Once our dad had all his kids in one room, nobody wanted a confrontation. Lamont was supposed to take the lead, but the right moment to do so just never came. We never got around to it and that's the way we left it. Thank God, too. Though we had intended to come there for an intervention, God intended for us to have harmony. This would be the last interaction we all had with him, and it was beautiful. Our dad was happy, and so were we.

He died of a massive heart attack just three months after that visit. The day was normal. Like every day before it, he had gotten up from the breakfast table, put his plate in the sink, and walked out of the kitchen, expecting to take up his usual residence in his favorite reclining chair.

Moments later, while going about her own daily routine, making their king-sized bed, Altamease discovered him unresponsive on the floor, hidden by the height of the mattress. Attempts to resuscitate him using CPR were unsuccessful. There was no warning. He had not been sick. He was 73 years old.

If he could have picked it, I know that's how my dad would have wanted to die. He didn't like hospitals and he didn't want to go to a nursing home. He lived with this communicated fear of dying alone with no one willing to take care of him.

Losing a loved one unexpectedly is like watching a movie, a cliffhanger, that ends in an abrupt way that you weren't prepared for. Like good cliffhangers, the writer, our Creator, had left us with many questions unanswered during what seemed like the climax of the narrative. What I know for sure is God assures us that there is a reason for every season and every purpose. He never promised He would tell us all the answers. He is the answer.

I had never lost a father before. The best way for me to describe the feeling is that we felt as though we had been stuck in a movie...a cliffhanger. I decided to take a master class on cliffhangers to make sense of this ending—of my father's life, of my hope of things ever being any different for me, for him, for my mothers, my sisters, or my brother.

As I grappled with losing my father and how to move my life forward, I decided that if this cliffhanger would be how his story would end, then our lives had to bear the fruits of a good sequel. *Writer's Digest*[1] offers several characteristics from which I found inspiration:

1. Good sequels have to be willing to let beloved characters go.

2. Good sequels have to tell the rest of the story.

3. Good sequels must be able to stand on their own.

But writing a sequel is not like writing a series. My siblings and our children are the series that our parents wrote. We have to write the sequel so people can see what happens next and ask for a follow-up to the narrative we leave behind.

Our father was the king of writing a letter to communicate all that he wanted to express. It is time now that we do the same.

We are the sequel. A good one. Our legacy continues....

[1]"Writing Sequels: 7 Rules for Writing Second Installments," *writersdigest.com/write-better-fiction/7-rules-writing-sequels*

A Hard Lesson in Becoming a Leader

Until the eighth grade, I attended a Seventh-day Adventist school in New Orleans' Lower Ninth Ward. Since the school only went to the tenth grade, my mom allowed me to transfer before high school began. My brother had challenges transitioning from the tenth grade there to high school. Not wanting me to experience similar issues, she consented to let me go to a public high school, even though she really didn't want me to do that. What she really wanted was to send me to a boarding school where I could continue receiving a Seventh-day Adventist education. To this day, I'll never understand how being educated within a religion was more important to her than me being home during those critical teenage years, but maybe the next few years would really tell that story.

Uncle Jimmy, my mother's only brother, was going to pay for it. James "Jimmy" Graham lived in Topeka, Kansas, and didn't have children of his own until later in life. For a long time, we were his children and remained so even after he had his own. He got married when I was five years old and I was the flower girl at their wedding. Uncle Jimmy was quite close to Mom and provided us with the things we wanted or needed.

Despite my uncle's generous offer, I didn't want to leave my friends to go to boarding school. My neighborhood friends were all applying to either John F. Kennedy High School or a new high school, Sarah T. Reed, being built in our neighborhood. I asked my mom if I could apply to JFK, which housed a magnet school within its program, but since we lived outside of its zoning, I had to test in to be admitted.

My friends and I caught the bus together and filed into the auditorium for all-day testing to gain entrance into the magnet consortium at John F. Kennedy High School. Going there to take the test was my first time seeing the school. I didn't know what it was about. I just knew that all my friends were going there, and so I wanted to go, too. This would be my first opportunity to go to school with kids from my neighborhood and to know the names in the stories they talked about on the playground. Before now, my interactions were limited to whoever came into the complex to visit and being on the outside of inside information, and even that was after I finished my homework and made it out to the playground positioned just below our third-floor apartment window.

The letters started coming in the mail, and everybody was finding out whether they got accepted or rejected. I was the only one among my group of friends to get accepted. And just as fast as they all decided that they were going to Kennedy, the decision was made to go to Reed. Naturally, I just as casually went to my mom and renounced my plans to attend the school I had just convinced her to allow me to test into.

"Mom, I want to go to Sarah T. Reed."

"No, you said you wanted to go to Kennedy with the rest of your friends."

"Well, none of them got in, so I don't want to go there now. I want to go where all of them are going," I explained, hoping she'd understand.

She was adamant. "This is going to be your first lesson in following your friends."

This was a tough lesson about being a follower, and I think what ultimately led me to be a leader who is careful to forge my own path. Some lessons are hard learned but stick like grits, and you know now how much I hate those!

My mom made me go to John F. Kennedy where I knew no one, and I wasn't prepared for that. The students were different from me. They came from a different walk of life. I was scared out of my mind.

Lamont dressed me for the first day of school. I should have gone to the school he attended, but I so didn't want to go to school with my brother. I wanted to get away from him because I didn't want to be Lamont's little sister for once in my life. That was my convincing argument for my mom letting me apply to a different school.

Lamont attended Warren Easton, a college prep school. The preppy kids who attended there dressed like the Catholic school kids who attended St. Augustine, the top Black Catholic school for boys. Often you couldn't tell a St. Aug boy from a Warren Easton boy because they dressed the same.

In New Orleans, Catholic schools offered a premiere education. In middle school, people thought I went to a Catholic school because I wore a uniform, as Catholic school students did. You could tell what school they went to based on their uniform's pattern.

Lamont picked out my clothes, sure that he knew what would be good for the first day. He selected a long Kelly green dress for me that came down to my ankles. The bibbed top buttoned at the shoulders and I wore a nautical printed button-up underneath. The high-waisted dress was pleated to the hem that was met by white stockinged feet in white pleather flats. I had worn a uniform for so many years, I had no idea what it meant to pick out clothes for school. I had no idea that this outfit selection would welcome or reject me into a clique from day one.

I remember it so vividly. I arrived on the schoolyard twenty or thirty minutes before the first bell with a paper schedule in hand. The school I had come from, with sixty students at most from kindergarten to tenth grade, had two bells, one in the morning to start the day and one at dismissal. Now here I was in entering a school with hundreds of students, several buildings, and seven classes. I barely even knew how I got here—the only time I had caught the bus to this part of town was when I came to test. I was lost and desperate to find some help.

I walked timidly and uncertain over to the fence where a lot of students had gathered to watch the marching band practice before school started. Ours was an amazing marching one hundred that stepped with precision across the student parking lot every morning before school, practicing field formations.

It took a lot of courage for me to do what would come next, but I had no idea how I would survive if I didn't get help to understand how to read this schedule or understand where I was supposed to be. Scared, I mustered the courage to ask a girl standing next to me if she knew where my class was or how to read this paper schedule in my hand. The girl, who wore a red pair of name-brand glasses, had a stylish cut in the '90s we called stacks. Hers were symmetrical layered cuts that were stiffened by at least a half bottle of hair spray that would have kept its shape for at least that first week. She wore baggy Girbaud jeans layered on top of at least one pair of basketball shorts and an oversized polo over another two undershirts to hide her thin frame. Extending my hand to show her my first block of classes, she turned her head toward me to drink in my green dress. Her long slow glance from my toes to my head and then back to the field where the band was practicing, said "Do not talk to me," even though she spoke no words. Humiliated and trying not to let tears fall from my face, I filed into the school not knowing what I would do next just as the first bell rang on the first day of ninth grade.

Because God loves me so much, even though I didn't recognize it then, he sent me an angel. My brother, John Calvin, was starting there that year, too. He wasn't a brother by blood, but he and Lamont were best friends and he too had attended Ephesus Junior Academy where I had. John later came to live with us for some time and was integrated into our home as if he was one of my mother's own children. That day, he would save me.

"John, where am I supposed to go?" I said, feeling relieved that I had seen a friendly face. He directed me to the cafeteria and added one more piece of advice before he went off to class.

"Don't let Lamont dress you tomorrow," he advised, shaking his head and reassuring me it would be all right.

The friends I went to high school with still laugh about my first day there. Keeva, the girl in the red glasses and baggy clothes, turned out to be one of the best friends I would carry, or who would carry me, depending on which season we are in, for the rest of my life. We got in trouble together in math class, caught the bus home down Haynes, and pooled our transfer money for fifteen cents buttermilk drop donuts from McKenzie's. We went to Xavier University together, both clueless about what we would become there. What we found out during our second semester was that she'd be there for me like a coach in the stirrups on her nineteenth birthday, the day I delivered my baby boy in a New Orleans East Hospital, January 7, 1993.

You Don't Want to Go Down that Road

My mother emphasized the importance of education. Her mantra was: "You better not bring a C in this house unless it's vitamins, and when you grow up you can be anything you want to be as long as it's a doctor, a lawyer, or a teacher."

In our community, aspirations to be doctors, lawyers, and teachers had an unspoken value. Though nobody ever spoke these words to me specifically, I somehow believed that's what we could do to be successful.

That's all I knew. I didn't know of any other professions I could pursue that would help me make lots of money and be successful. No one ever told me that I could be anything else and still be a success.

I was smart, and I was ambitious. I was going to be a doctor.

I wanted to help people, and that's the way I thought you helped people, by becoming a doctor. I had never really been to the hospital, and besides checkups, that by my teenage years were only for sporadic vaccinations, I had barely even been in a doctor's office. What I did believe, and no one confirmed this for me either, was that doctors drove nice cars, lived in huge fancy houses, and had spouses and children who loved them. I didn't particularly have any interest in medicine other than physicians. They were considered smart, they were heard, listened to, and respected, and the idea of it would be pleasing to the adults in my life. Besides, all the really smart kids I knew were throwing around these same aspirations.

I was determined to pursue medicine, so much so that I did it all—summer camps at Xavier, Bio Star the summer before tenth grade, and Chem Star the summer before the eleventh—to prepare me to shine when I enrolled at Xavier University in the fall, right after my seventeenth birthday.

Since I'd finished high school a year early, I stepped onto Xavier's campus not knowing what college was. Honestly, even had I taken an extra year at Kennedy, I still would have stepped into college not knowing what to expect. I had never visited one, didn't explore opportunities that any had to offer, and didn't even know what was really expected of me when I got there except to do like my mother had required, keep my grades up. In fact, I only went to college early because my mother had gotten a job promotion that would be moving our family to Tulsa, Oklahoma, in my senior year. I didn't want to go to a new school, in a new place, in my senior year, and she didn't want to leave me behind with friends. My father lived in New Orleans, but I didn't want to live with him. His house was on the West Bank, away from everything I knew; plus, my dad was extremely strict. I was dreading what living in my father's house again would mean. My younger sisters would have loved for me to move in with them, and they had room for me to come there.

In high school, I had a teacher who was doing his dissertation at Xavier, and I told him about my situation—I didn't want to leave New Orleans and I didn't want to go to a new school. He suggested that I apply to go directly to college and skip my senior year. I was going to be the valedictorian of my class, based on my grades up to that point, and I only needed one class to graduate. To keep valedictorian status, I had to take four classes, and I didn't want to do that. I took an English class I needed that summer. The school administration said I could come back and graduate with my class the following year. I finished high school in August 1991, and I went back to attend graduation with my class in 1992. I was sixteen when I finished high school in May, and I turned seventeen on July 4. Thinking back, that's too young to be making those kinds of decisions, but I think our society puts so much pressure on children to be "grown."

I didn't know what it took to get into college. I didn't know what it meant to fill out financial aid applications. Although my brother had gone to college, he was the first and my mom's crash course in sending her children off to school. I had vowed not to do whatever that was to my mom. I watched her send all her extras and stay on her knees believing God would help her help him. So, she couldn't really help me.

My mother also didn't want me to go away to school, because I was her baby, and I was young. I felt like I didn't really have a say in where I was going to enroll. She had wanted me to go away to boarding school to finish high school, but she didn't want me to go away to college. So I went to Xavier, a small Catholic school where my professor had connections, and he got me a scholarship.

I was desperate to stay in New Orleans with all my friends. I had visited the high school in Tulsa, and I didn't want to be a senior there. As it turned out, my mother didn't leave New Orleans. She worked it out so that she was able to work from home. By that time, I had my heart set on higher education, and I had told everybody I was going to college early. I didn't want to backtrack and stay in high school.

I lived at home with my mother, but she traveled a lot. My next-door neighbors kept an eye out for me, and they weren't worried about me because I was a responsible kid.

I caught the bus to the campus some days. On other days I drove my mom's car or sometimes I would carpool with my girlfriends if my mom was in town and needed her car.

Once I started my classes, I found that no pre-med, pre-college science program could have prepared me for what high school couldn't offer me. I couldn't apply the science no matter how much I applied myself. I was in danger of losing my scholarship and not sure how I would pay for college if I was a science major who couldn't balance chemical equations.

I didn't even know what it took to be a doctor. I didn't know where medical schools were located. I did know I was going to have to take the MCAT eventually. But since standardized tests and I didn't fare well, I never really explored what it took to take that.

I considered my options. I was good at French, and I enjoyed that. I was passionate about the language at the time, and I was excelling in the class. Nobody who looks like me really speaks French fluently, and I always wanted to stand out. People told me, "You should study Spanish because that's a language skill that is usable."

"My name doesn't say that I should speak Spanish," I thought. "With a name like Mignon, I should be speaking French." I picked up speaking the language really well after I started taking conversational French in high school. By the time I was in college, it was an easy grade for me.

I quickly decided that I would become a translator, thinking it would be cool to get paid for speaking and interpreting another language. When I shared my plans with my mom, she told me there was no future in that and no money in it either. My mom was controlling the narrative.

After discouraging my dream, Mom commanded that I focus more on my studies. Instead, I focused on the college parties. After one epic party too many, I soon found myself pregnant at age seventeen. I entered my sophomore year with a belly bump.

Looking back, I know that I got pregnant because I was heartbroken. My boyfriend was a DJ who worked all the campus parties. He was an older student and veteran who was using his GI Bill to go to school. He was attractive and he drove a gold BMW. We did everything together, but eventually I found out that he was also messing around with one of the girls that I went to church with. One of my friends told him, "If you don't tell her, I will."

The discovery of his unfaithfulness plummeted my self-esteem even more. I already believed I was never pretty enough or never had the right clothes. His shenanigans left me heartbroken.

On Valentine's Day, he showed up at one of my classes holding gigantic balloons, some flowers and, among other things, a can of SlimFast. My feelings were already hurt, but he thought it was funny. I wasn't feeling his brand of love. I promptly broke up with him and refused all his advances toward reconciliation. I refused to answer his phone calls. He even showed up at our front door one day. I slammed the door in his face.

I went home after his Valentine's Day stunt and buried my head in the giant, pillowy fortress of my mother's overstuffed plush sofa. I was sad and heartbroken. My sister Michelle had been seeing a guy she had become acquainted with through me. He had been a customer of mine that I met at my after-school shoe store job at The Plaza in New Orleans. She was too young to be exchanging numbers with him, but that never stopped anything. There to pick her up for a date, he noticed me looking pitiful. "You shouldn't be sad on Valentine's Day," he told me. He offered to call his cousin Troy to see if he wanted to go out with me. I remembered meeting his cousin one Thanksgiving at one of their family functions and thought he was cute. I thought it pretty promising that he might be feeling me too since moments later I was in the car heading to hang out with them at the bowling alley.

Troy had way too much swag for me, to be honest. He was worldly and much too experienced, but he had a fancy car and a bad-boy attitude. Frankly, he could've been a leaping lizard that day, I just needed to be wanted.

Guided by my broken heart I plunged into a situation that was doomed from the outset. Here's what I knew about him: He lived with a woman, and they were expecting a child. I gathered that watching his mother announce to the family that she was going to be a grandmother. I was drawn to the way his legs bowed in the center and the really nice car I saw him pull up and drive off in, I found him to be attractive, with a flare his family seemed fond of. Even though I knew he belonged to someone. I started seeing him anyway. What in the world was I thinking? I would meet him in hotels—like he was my boyfriend, like I knew what I was doing, like I liked what I was getting—and then go home.

Only, I wasn't a woman. Mentally and emotionally, I was a child in a woman's body who had no business hooking up with a twenty-three-year-old man in a hotel room. The consequence of my secret rendezvous was a pregnancy I was poorly equipped to deal with.

It's only now, thirty years older with a lot of therapy sessions under my belt, that I'm becoming a woman who knows what I want

Recipe Note to My Younger Self...

You don't want to go down that road, Mignon, and here's why: If you go down that road, and you refuse to listen to what God is telling you to do, you'll get caught up in the wrong crowd of people. Next thing you know, you'll find yourself in a hotel room with a man who's telling you, "Oh, you going to give me that... Oh, you're not a woman?"

and who knows when God is speaking to her: "This is what I want you to do now. This is what I want you to do next. Stop doing that. I'm going to help you. I'm going to lead you. I'm going to speak to you." God's messages are always a lifeline for me.

It's like oxygen for me to breathe, and often compels me to tell others, "That little voice on the inside that's telling you, 'You're not supposed to be here.' That's God speaking. Forget what everybody else is saying or what everybody else wants you to do. That little desire, that little fire that you feel, that's God telling you, 'You don't belong here. I have so much more for you to do.'" I share this with people because if nobody ever tells you, how are you ever supposed to know what you can be, what you can make, what you can do?

I remember the first time I heard God speak and I knew without a doubt it was a divine message meant for me. Somehow, I knew what it was then. Though I heard it clearly and a small swarm of butterflies met up in my stomach to convict me, younger me was a Wonder Woman who could use her cuffs to deflect whatever got thrown my way. And even though I never activated those cuffs or used an invisible plane to get me out of those uncomfortable places I knew I shouldn't be, I do know now that was the Holy Spirit trying his best to activate. I heard it before I ever chose to get in the car that drove me to the other side of town to meet the guy who never really even chose me: "Now, you don't have no business going there, Mignon."

I responded to the Spirit speaking to me, "Well, I'm over him, anyway. I'm just going to prove to him that I'm over him."

I hadn't talked to Troy in a month, but I saw him on the highway, and he flagged me down. When he suggested a hotel, I agreed because I wanted him to know that I wasn't thinking about him. Just a couple minutes in the door, however, he was on top of me. I didn't even know how to enjoy that moment, if indeed it was meant for me to enjoy. I just knew that I wanted to be wanted. I wanted to be liked. I wanted to be chosen. I wanted somebody to see me.

I'm still looking for those things, except now I know that there are certain things I have that nobody else has—traits that make me unique, that make me desirable, that make me worthy of winning.

When I think back on my relationship with Troy, he was never mine, never really my boyfriend. He was someone I wanted to want me. I stopped seeing him or even talking to him after that encounter. That would be the last time... until it wasn't. That year, 1992, taught me a lot of lessons about who I was becoming and who I wanted to be. I was learning my way around campus, but I watched from the sidelines as members of the Black Greek-letter groups stomped the yard, and I was failing miserably at college chemistry, in the lab, and in love. Not really ready for what college had to offer, I was burning the candle at both ends.

Xavier's campus was abuzz over the upcoming All Nighter, a party my then-ex would DJ. Guys dapping each other off as they crossed the yard, black glossy fliers slapped into our hands that shimmered with gold and the promise of drinking and dancing all night, all for the student-budget price of twenty dollars. I dragged myself out, tagging along with a few upperclassmen girls I had known from high school who now granted me the privilege of hanging around them. I didn't have anything to drink, not even water. The smell of liquor was enticing to me, but the taste was musky. Besides that, I was underage. The hot room spun like records on a turntable to the beat of '90s hip hop music that moved the crowd. The Greeks stepped, strolled, shimmied, and set out the hops.

I was doing my own sort of strolling, walking in the house that late, but I got by undetected until the sound of hurling sent my mother into the hall bathroom, where I curtsied low at the porcelain throne just on the side of the tub. I never got sick, and I never threw up, but there I was spilling my guts into the toilet and praying that God would let it stop. There was a full-on flu epidemic and children were dying. A friend of my cousin's had died of the flu just weeks earlier. Feeling weak and faint, I took up residence on the sofa where my mom fed me things like soup and apples that I just couldn't hold down. With just about all the color drained from my body, and with all the vomiting, I could barely move. Mom told me, "You need to see the doctor about the flu." That's all I thought it was, but that was literally enough to scare me right off the couch and into the doctor's office where I went for normal pediatric care. I think that's all the doctor thought it was too, at first.

After examining me, the doctor disappeared from the room with a couple of swabs in hand and a promise to be back. When she came back in, she said, "You don't have the flu. You're pregnant, honey." I was in shock, and I can still see the room. It was a sunny day. She was a white doctor. She had never met me before. I was sitting on the edge of the exam table with my feet dangling, waiting for her to come back with prescriptions for the flu. She sat by my side, put her hand on my lap, and immediately started the intake process for what I needed to know now about having a baby. She reassured me that there were options, and asked me if I knew who the father was, to which I responded, "I don't do the things you have to do to be pregnant."

She said nothing.

I was a hot mess. I was seventeen years old, sitting on the exam table in a doctor's office telling her, a medical professional with years of experience, "I can't be pregnant because I don't have sex."

I was serious. I didn't even know how to get pregnant. And seriously, not to shirk personal responsibility, I just believed that me getting pregnant wasn't possible. I had heard it could happen after just one time. It just never occurred to me that it could actually happen to me. And let me add, had I believed he was truly my boyfriend and had he taken me places and treated me with care, then I could have imagined the possibility that we could create a baby together. But with the way things were set up, I was not prepared. I felt like I been duped. I never got asked on a date, was never taken to a show, never paraded in public, and never frolicked under covers or lay in his arms for hours engaging in small talk. That's what they did on the soap opera stories my grandmother loved. Was that stupid? Was I that clueless? So, since I never got those things, how could I be pregnant? Don't you have to be naked to get pregnant?

When the clinic doctor entered the examination room, her face had a knowing concern that smeared her face like a death mask. I can't remember if I begged her or simply tried to persuade her through my maturity or my innocence, but I began pleading with that doctor, "You must have gotten my tests mixed up with somebody else's!"

Her stoic gaze never changed. All she could offer me was a knowing look that told me, "I know this is hard for you."

"I don't even have sex!" I continued to challenge her diagnosis.

She got a box of tissues and set it on the exam table. "I have the right test," she spoke gently, but with authority.

All my pleadings and rationalizations to convince her to check again fell on deaf ears. She was even a little perturbed at the inference that she had made a mistake. I was so sure she had this all wrong. I desperately wanted her to be wrong.

"Take all the time you need to absorb the news," she gave her parting words of consolation. "Stop by my receptionist's desk and she can give you referrals to…." She rattled off a string of initials and acronyms I had never heard of that could help me whether I kept my baby, or by any means necessary, not.

I sat there for a while until I had to go. I took a seat in the lobby and waited a while before going up to the receptionist. "Is there no way I can get a second opinion?" I winced. The person behind the counter shuffled some papers toward me. I barely looked at them. I didn't want to need those papers. I didn't even want to look at them. I was in silent panic mode. Shock! I don't remember how I walked out of that office, but I eventually got to the car. I still remember with great clarity the route I took home down Lake Forest Boulevard through the neighborhood. The drive was slow and silent.

I had no one I could tell. My friends were not even having sex. Were they even kissing boys? I had never felt more alone, and as I rolled to a halt at the four-way stop, I yelled out to God, "Whyyyyyy meeeee?!" I pounded the steering wheel, but no answer came, just a honk from the driver behind me, nudging me to keep it moving. And that's precisely what I did. I didn't have a choice because the world would keep moving whether I was pregnant or not.

I felt I had been robbed. The more I thought about it, I began to realize that I had been robbed of so much in my life. I really felt like crying. I was robbed of so much in my life by men who wanted to use my body, and I didn't know what it was. I didn't know what I had.

The first thing I knew to do was call my sister, Michelle. "You need to get off work," I told her.

It was easy for me to confide in her because she was beyond scolding me anymore. By this time, she was more like a best friend. My other sisters were only seven and twelve at the time, so I commandeered Michelle for the duty, and there she has remained.

I drove to her job, and she came outside, opened the passenger door, and plopped down in the front seat next to me. I handed her the papers the doctor had given me.

She blurted out, "Are you pregnant?"

"That's what the papers say."

She immediately started giving me strategies of what I needed to do. Because she had gotten pregnant at nineteen, she had experience with this kind of situation. "This is what you're going to do.... This is what you're going to say...."

I was scared to tell my mom. Actually, I was more than scared. I was terrified.

"All right, I'm going to go with you," Michelle offered.

When we got to the house, I was trying to act as normal as possible, so as not to arouse Mom's suspicions.

My mom was working in her office, and Michelle and I came and stood in the doorway. "What did you do, and why are you standing there looking stupid?" My mom knew her girls.

It was so scary. Michelle didn't say anything, and I didn't say anything, but I felt hot on the inside.

"Would you say something? Why are you girls standing there just staring at me?" Mom knew something wasn't right.

Michelle finally broke. "Mignon has something to tell you."

"What?"

I tried to get it out, but I couldn't talk. My mom looked at my sister and asked, "Michelle, are you pregnant?" She giggled and added, "That's the only thing y'all can be standing here for looking stupid."

"No, but Mignon is." I was grateful Michelle had told the dreaded news for me.

My mom was holding some orange binders full of paper, and they dropped out of her hands to the table with a thud. Her hands were still suspended in midair as she began to scream.

"I would have put my head on a chopping block to say 'Not my daughter!'" she raged pounding the table with every syllable.

Her hands finally dropped to the desk below them. She rose from her chair and walked away without saying a word. She didn't speak to me for a week. She would walk past me in the house in silence. I think at some point she may have asked me who was the father, because as far as she knew I didn't even have a boyfriend.

Finally, the day came when she broke the silence. I guess when she became ready to deal with me and my situation, she called me from her phone at work. "Do you have a pen?" she spewed. "Write this number down." She talked at me in a brash, gruff way that made me wince with every word.

I wrote the number down and called it. It was the abortion hotline. She told me to listen to everything that the voice on the other end had to say and then call her back. So, I listened. The automated voice talked about pregnancy about the various stages of gestation. That day I was amazed by two things: one that my mother made me call the abortion hotline, and secondly that a baby gets its personality ten days after conception. I had a human growing inside of me and it had already been determined what that person would be like. I remember that phone call ending with an unassured confused feeling of wondering what I was doing there. I couldn't believe what I was hearing. After listening to the information, I cried. How could she want me to kill a baby?

I called Mom back. "Mom, you told me to call the abortion clinic. How could you do that? Aren't you a Christian? Aren't you the one who tells everybody else to do the right thing?" That's what my mom was for me—a moral compass. In fact, she was everything to everybody's situation. All the teenagers at church and in the neighborhood looked up to my mother, the Sabbath school teacher. They confided in her for wise counsel.

Yet this was the same woman who gave me the number to the abortion clinic. She listened to me unload on her. Then she said, "I just wanted you to know that you had a human being inside of you and that abortion would be killing."

That was the first conversation we had about my pregnancy, and that was the beginning of us figuring out what we were going to do. It was awkward for my mom to be a part of my pregnancy because I was embarrassed that I had gotten pregnant and that I had brought this shame to our family.

Mom called my dad to come over. I thought, "What is he coming over here for?"

I was devastated. When he got there, he actually spoke to me calmly. I don't remember exactly what he said, but it was something like, "It's going to be all right. I'm going to help you. Whatever you need us to do. Your parents are here for you."

I think that was the first time I clearly saw my father's love for me, the kind of paternal protection I was longing to obtain through a meaningless sexual encounter. My pregnancy affected him deeply. "I feel like God is punishing me through you," he confessed, "for all the things I've done in my life. He's paid it back with you."

My parents immediately jumped in to see what they could do to fix my problem. My father even offered to adopt the baby so I could continue with school.

"You are not going to adopt my baby," I thought. "I love my baby." I didn't know him yet, but I certainly didn't want my father to adopt him.

My dad's motives were pure, though. He wanted to do it so he could provide my child with health insurance and other things that I wouldn't be able to give him right away.

I was unmoved. "Absolutely not."

My mother and father were trying to be as supportive as they knew how to be. Dad wanted to excommunicate whoever the daddy was. "We can be all the family that baby needs."

I called Troy to tell him that I was pregnant the day I found out. He asked me who the father was.

"What do you mean whose baby is it?" I was a good girl. I wouldn't have sex with just anybody, but Troy was living with somebody who had a miscarriage, and he couldn't let some seventeen-year-old girl come in and ruin his life.

"What are you going to do?" Troy asked.

"What do you mean what am I going to do? I'm going to keep my baby!"

I didn't even tell him when I had the baby because he had rejected me during the whole pregnancy. I ran into him when I was about seven or eight months pregnant, even bigger and wobbling. I spotted his car near a Walgreens drug store. There was a girl sitting inside and I was ready to fight. I drove my car around a circle and parked it next to his. I walked to his car and started banging on his hood. By the time I'd gotten to the car, the girl had gone into the drug store and was coming out with diapers. I was thinking, "Seriously, dude? You're taking care of this chick, and you won't even acknowledge me?"

"I'm going to call you later. Go home," he told me.

I sat by that phone, but he never called. It was then that I decided I wasn't going to let him know when the baby was born.

I do not have many pictures of me during that first pregnancy because nobody was proud of that. Nobody was proud that I was seventeen years old, unmarried, not in a relationship, and having a baby. Nobody documented my pregnancy journey, including the man whose baby I was having. I was embarrassed, too. I was embarrassed for any of my family members to see me pregnant because I couldn't hide what I had done. I do have a picture taken that Christmas of me playing Nintendo. My belly's not in the picture. You can see that I'm holding this thing up on my stomach. That was just days before I delivered my baby.

When I look at my face then, I look like I'm about twelve years old and I wonder, "How did somebody want sex from me?" The picture is evidence that I was a baby having a baby.

Dillon was born in New Orleans on January 7, 1993, despite the fact that I wasn't prepared to be a mother. I think I have always been looking to be chosen for something, to be accepted, to be wanted by somebody. In my younger years, I was always looking for that in the wrong places. I didn't get what I was looking for; I got a baby. I think that of all the things that I could have received, a baby is the best.

When I look back on my first pregnancy and who my son has become, I am very proud. He has loved me beyond what I deserve.

If I had to go back and do it all again, I would, just to be his mom. Dillon has been such a godsend to me. He's kind. He's smart. We grew up together. I very much grew up as I raised my own baby.

I'm glad I made the decision to keep my baby. I had to get welfare assistance to take care of him, and I applied for everything I could get. I didn't know anything about these things. Somehow my mother made too much money to receive any kind of assistance for anything, yet I didn't have money for anything. I didn't know how to work the system that I so desperately needed, but I never wanted to be a victim in my life, so I always looked at the situation as God never allowing me to figure out the system because He didn't want me to get swallowed into it. He didn't want me to stay there. I used the system for as long as I could use it and for what I needed to use it .

I learned to breastfeed my baby because I could afford that. I learned to stack milk from the WIC office, planning for the day that would come when he might need formula. I also had daycare assistance because I was in college full time.

Brian, the cousin who introduced Troy to me, knew when I had the baby and came to see him. The baby looked just like Troy. He said, "My aunt (Troy's mother) is going to be so excited that she has a grandbaby. Don't you at least want to tell her?"

I didn't know what his mother would think. I didn't know her.

Brian told Troy anyway. A few days later, Troy and his father came by the house. I guess he brought his dad because he was nervous. My dad and mom were there, and they started asking him questions.

"Who are you? Where do you work? What are you doing?"

They were trying to find out who these people were. When my parents left, Troy said he felt attacked, but I felt protected by my dad. They weren't happy about the circumstances, but I also know that my dad was excited about his first grandchild.

"How dare you?" he raged at me about my father asking him all those questions. My parents had every right to ask those questions about their daughter and this baby. I was just eighteen, he was twenty-three.

When Troy saw him, he knew that Dillon was his baby. Actually, he knew it when I told him I was pregnant. There was no question, at least in my mind, because I had not had relations with anyone else. He asked me if we could take the baby to meet his mom. I agreed to take Dillon to meet his paternal grandmother.

His mom had no clue a baby was coming, and she cried when she saw him. She couldn't believe there was a baby connected to her that she knew nothing about. "I never was going to tell you," I confessed, "because I had heard stories about girls knocking on doors saying, 'This is your grandbaby' and being rejected."

His mother said, "A mother knows, Mignon. A mother knows."

She connected to baby Dillon, and he was everything to her. As soon as I would let her, she started picking Dillon up and spending the entire day with him. She learned how to drive so she could be with her grandbaby. She knew her son wasn't doing things he needed to do, so she started providing financial assistance to help me take care of the baby. She would give me money—maybe one hundred or two hundred dollars—every month. That was a lot of money in 1992. She would put money in a bank account for Dillon and make sure that he had diapers. She would often pick him up on Saturdays, and he would come back home with brand-new clothes, diapers, and other things. She loved Dillon and she continued to provide support for him until I got married when he was thirteen months old.

The Baker's Man

"Pat-a-cake, Pat-a-cake, Baker's Man.
Bake me a cake as fast as you can."

I met the man who would become my husband at orientation when I transferred to Our Lady of Holy Cross College in 1994. He kind of stalked me around campus for a couple of weeks. Eventually, I told my mom about him. "There's a guy that I think likes me at school, but I think he's old. He must be at least twenty-nine!"

His name was Alvin François. I always called him François because my dad's name was Alvin, and it felt weird to call my father and my husband by the same name.

I had transferred to Holy Cross, a small Catholic school in New Orleans, with the idea of gaining a spot in their nursing school program to make a better life for me and my son. I had wanted to be a doctor, but the years required for medical school would have to wait. I needed something a lot quicker than that, and soon my marriage to a man with three of his own children, and our resulting financial struggles, would soon make me postpone my dreams of being a nurse, too.

Located just a few blocks from the Mississippi River on the West Bank of the city in Algiers, Holy Cross was snuggled amongst sprawling green grass and old oak trees that offer their shade to anyone privileged to be in their company. One day after class, I slid into my car, a 1986 four-door, metallic gray Chevy Cavalier with a pin-stripe detail that had made it a little extra special to my mother. I remember my mom negotiating to have that stripe added without an extra cost. The salesman threw it in to sweeten the deal. The gray velour seats were pristine, and the car usually presented as clean since the color could easily hide dirt and stains. That's why Mom had picked that color. The Cavalier was really Mom's car, but I say it was mine because it was in my possession most of the time. My mother worked around my schedule to make the car available for me, but my son Dillon and I did catch the bus from time to time if she needed the car.

Since Dillon was in daycare on the East Bank of New Orleans where we lived, I often took the ferry boat home for a break from the reality of the day. On the short ride across the river, the muddy waters churning beneath the boat were always enough to take my mind off the turmoil in my life. Mostly, I prayed from one riverbank to the other that we wouldn't drown in that rage of the mighty Mississippi. On this particular day, I was going to take a nap on the ride across, pick up my baby early, and take him to the park to enjoy the nice January weather. I daydreamed about how excited his little face would be to see me. In New Orleans, January could be warm sometimes, and I remember this day being the kind of weather where you could roll your car windows down and enjoy a welcome break from the usual winter snap. I mostly remember it, though, because as I sat in my car, waiting to drive onto the ferry, I was awakened from my daydream by the sound of a roaring engine coming alongside me onto the levee, a luscious green grass mound that lined the rivers banks to hold the water back from drowning our city.

The driver's window was rolled all the way down, and he perched his left arm on the ledge of his vintage Cadillac car. A "classic car" was what he called it. It was an old, rickety thing to me, and I was unimpressed as he hung out of the window flashing a bright, wide-toothed smile across his chiseled square face. His left arm was darkened a few shades more, like burnt caramel, from his habitual perch on the window—not because he enjoyed resting it there, but rather, because it was the only way to condition the air on the inside of that tank he called a collectible. I was honestly taken aback, even a little bit scared. Was he stalking me? No, he was literally chasing me. I was sure of it. I had seen him a few times before.

Now, as I waited for the ferry, seeing him was a little creepy and a little exciting, I guess. I was a naïve nineteen-year-old with a little baby at home, no boyfriend, and no prospects.

I waved to him and decided the wait for the ferry would be longer than I wanted today. I should have seen the signs then, but I digress.

The first time I remembered seeing him was on that earlier orientation day. I had been nervous to be starting this new journey where I didn't know anyone. Plus, I was changing my major to nursing, something I knew nothing about. What I did know was this was the school that could get me there, or that's what I'd heard. I was once again pursuing something I had only heard others talk about without knowing anything about what it would actually take to make it real for me.

I was late walking into the crowded cafeteria/auditorium to attend orientation for transfer students and freshman. The sterile, bright white room was packed with eager students looking in the direction of the financial aid officer, who was giving instructions for the morning. All eyes turned toward me as I interrupted their attention. I tried to be quiet, but I clumsily caused the door to slam behind me and caught the robotic turn of heads from the entire room. I scanned their faces, looking for any sign of familiarity or friendliness. There was none, except for one fair-skinned, square-faced guy who locked eyes with me across the room. He and I were the only Black people there. He seemed mesmerized. He stared, and I could feel beams of electricity burning a hole through my skin across the room. I was too shy to cast my gaze in his direction for very long. I winced and turned forward until the welcome session was over.

After orientation, I fumbled my way through the halls of the tiny school and made my way to the financial aid room. This place was nothing like the size of my previous college, Xavier University. "I should be able to conquer these halls," I thought. What made it so weird, though, was that as I waited for my turn to see the bursar, I turned to look at the other students in line. Some small talk picked up amongst the few chattering students who were obviously returning. There he was again. That light-skinned guy, the color of a peach crayon in the Crayola 24 box set. He was smiling directly at me. I turned my head back quickly, almost snapping my neck in whiplash, but he never stopped staring. There went those light beams again. This time they were bearing down on my back, and I knew I had to get out of there before he completely undressed me with his eyes.

I have always been shy, especially when it comes to meeting men. It was even more awkward because I could feel his eyes following me, undressing me on site. So, imagine my horror when he came chasing me down the hall one evening after I'd decided to dip out early from a statistics class. He had been watching me; no, let's call that studying me, from the open door of his night class. Across the hall from his class was a student lounge filled with snacks. I've always had a sugary sweet tooth, and this machine was loaded with Lance's mini pecan pies that reminded me of nearly everything I loved about childhood snacks. Each night, I visited the machine for a gooey, molasses-filled pie to devour as I walked to the car. This time, the stranger had positioned himself at his classroom door, next to the snack room. When he saw me pass by, he decided to make a move. All I heard were a jangling bunch of keys bounding down the hall in a cadence.

"You're new here," he said, smiling with a deep dimpled grin, spreading his square chiseled face. I was still clutching my things, afraid he was intending to steal from me. I really had no reason to think that, honestly. The school was a very safe place, but I did think that in the moment. He walked alongside me and asked my name. I can't remember whether it was on this occasion or our next encounter, but he thought it clever to inform me that I was going to be his wife. I was not swayed.

He walked me to the car and asked for my number. I gave it to him. We went our separate ways, though he kept looking back at me. Not paying attention to what was in front of him, he tripped over something and fell to the ground. I laughed.

I don't know why I gave him my number, except that he told me he was a tile contractor, and my mom had been talking for years about getting tile in our house. He wanted to come and give her a bid, so I gave the number to him. I immediately thought, "Why did I do that? I should have taken his number so my mom could call him."

He called to ask about the tiling job, and he was a good salesman. He persuaded her to let him come and give her a bid. He wanted the tile job, but he also wanted a date with me. He started the job at our house, and I would stay up with him at night while he worked on those floors. In the end, he wouldn't charge her for the job. She insisted on paying him, but he wouldn't take the money.

Alvin François was thirty years old and a father of three children. He had served in the military, and he was running his own business. Later, he told me he was going through a divorce and raising his children. I had no business in that space. I was in over my head and too young and naïve to know it.

Our whirlwind dating experience mixed with François' charm made it hard for me to realize that I wasn't equipped to play his game.

Over time, I came to recognize the man I married too quickly talked a good game he wasn't able to deliver a win on. He started selling me his $10,000-in-the-bank dream that sounded like security for a nineteen-year-old girl with a baby, no money, and no real grasp on what good money was. Until that point, my parents had provided everything for me, and I didn't even know how much money they made. All I knew is that everything I had went to the care of my baby and what was left I saved for him or what we would need in the future. All that hard work to scrimp and save had only garnered me $1,000 in an account marked for things I needed for Dillon, or for "someday," whichever day of the week that turned out to be. So the idea of having ten times that amount seemed like stability. And even though François claimed to have money in the bank, he somehow convinced me to let him have a $1,000 "someday" fund— my "someday" fund. He offered me a story and what seemed like a sure win to repay it, including doubling my money if he was late. At the end of his hard luck story, I had empathy for him. I also thought I could help him with the children and help them—"save" them, even though I was little more than a child myself.

I never saw that money. Honestly, at the time I had no real concept of the value of money and what it could do if handled or appropriated rightly, at least not yet. But I was about to find out.

I'm a person who looks for signs, and I thought the fact that his name was the same as my dad's was a sign. My parents had gotten engaged just four weeks after they met. Like my parents, François and I met and got engaged four weeks later. Three months later they were married. My dad had been in the military. François was a veteran as well. In my youthful, trusting mind, these were signs our relationship was meant to be. It seemed right. I chose not to think about the fact that my parents had divorced and that my father had been abusive toward my mother. Those should have been signs, too, but I did not know at the time how many ways my parents' relationship story would become my story, too.

When my mom saw François get on his knees to propose to me, she ran out of the room. "I can't take it," she said. In retrospect, I wish she had said, "No. You're not getting married to this man. This is not happening."

Now, I wish I could go back and shake my mom and tell her, "Lady, say 'no.' I'm your baby. I'm nineteen. I already have a baby from one relationship mistake. Just tell me, 'No, you're not marrying somebody who's thirty with three children.'"

But my mom stood by because it was too much like what she had done. It reminded her of her relationship with my dad, except my parents were the same age. She probably felt like she couldn't say much to me. What she did say was, "You know you don't have to do this." Even the day before my wedding, she told me, "Mignon, we can call this off."

"Mom, stop being so negative," I told her. "I'm getting married tomorrow."

I guess I thought, "I am grown, and I can make my own decisions." Still, I'm sure she could see signs of trouble to come in my relationship with François that I could not.

"You don't want to think about this, Mignon?" she asked me.

I don't know why she didn't at least try to put her foot down. So, getting no true opposition, I walked down the aisle, still a child in many ways, having no idea what I was getting into, marrying a man who knew exactly what he was doing.

I had convinced myself it was the thing to do, but in the days before it was time for me to walk down the aisle, I heard in my spirit, "Do not marry him. Do not marry him."

"There's no way I could call off the wedding," I thought. "People have bought gifts. They bought plane tickets. They're coming in town for a wedding. I can't call it off." As quickly as I heard that voice, I reasoned that I could not do what it was saying even though it was speaking very clearly.

Although he vowed to work really hard to make those things real, he had lied to me. The foundation of our relationship was built on the thing my father taught his children to detest most: dishonesty. Dear God, you know how my father hated liars. The harder thing was accepting that I was wrong and hadn't listened to the warnings. The hard thing was swallowing my pride and sucking up the I-told-you-so stories. I chose the road riddled with obstacles instead of doing the one simple thing: tell him the truth—I wasn't interested in marrying a man who could lie to me.

That's not, however, the way a nineteen-year-old thinks, and that's why most nineteen-year-olds probably shouldn't get married. Little did I know, those people would have been so happy to return those gifts or leave them, or say, "Keep it for yourself. I'm so happy

Recipe Note to My Younger Self...

The Holy Spirit's instructions are simple, but they are not necessarily easy. It would have been a simple task to walk right into that room and say, "I can't marry you." It would have been a simple task to say that to the person who, just moments before, had come clean and admitted that he could not provide the things he promised you.

you're not getting married." Those same people might have even come to town to celebrate a wedding that didn't take place.

The message I heard in my spirit, I later learned to know as the leading of the Holy Spirit. Though I didn't learn to listen on July 17, 1994, throughout the years, we would grow to be close pals.

Another motivating factor for me to go through with the wedding was that my brother had convinced me that no man would ever want to marry me because I already had a child. He taunted and sneered at the idea that I somehow believed a nice man would choose me and cherish me. Nobody ever reprimanded him for saying such things or encouraged him to think differently. While I had openly rejected his negative prophecies, I had silently accepted them as truth, along with so many other jabs my brother made toward me. I believed I was unworthy. I believed nobody else was going to want me, so I needed to take whatever man I could get. If this man wanted to marry me, I believed I should accept. That's exactly what I did.

We were married in my mom's backyard. The ink was barely dry on the divorce decree he'd gotten before the wedding, and our marriage came with a ready-made family—Alexius, seven; Lauren, five; Jacques, three; and my Dillon. After our wedding, I joined our instant family in an apartment we had secured a few months earlier, but not long afterward, we found ourselves struggling to keep our finances afloat. My mom had been wanting to convert her garage into an efficiency apartment, and François could do the work. With mom gone traveling for work most weeks, we moved into her converted garage, with children in tow, to save money.

A Lesson in Trusting God

While we were living in the garage at Mom's, I became pregnant with our daughter, Brittany (later named Druscilla). She was born in December 1995, a year and a half after we married. Being pregnant and married brought joy to my belly I hadn't experienced before. People wanted pictures. I could smile and happily discuss my progress. I could proudly wear my big baby bump in public.

My mother was not happy that I was pregnant. To this day, I don't know why, but most likely it was because we didn't have much money and we were living in her house. Her reaction was only slightly different from when I'd gotten pregnant as a teenager, and that really hurt my feelings. I understood why she wasn't happy when I got pregnant as a teenager, but this time I had a husband. I didn't get it. (Years later, my mother wasn't happy when I got pregnant with Xavier, but neither was I.)

Pregnancy with a loving partner who wants the baby just as much as you do is so much more rewarding than fighting to be acknowledged and being left alone with turmoil that it took two to create. My husband always wanted to come along to participate.

Our doctor visits were always routine. I dressed up for the visits and often wore a bucket hat accented by a flower. During pregnancy I figured there were enough odds against me to not add looking frumpy to the mix. When we went for the ultrasound, we were excited about getting to know our baby a little bit better.

The tech smeared the jelly all over my belly and snapped pictures and made measurements as the active little baby—that we had just learned was a girl—flipped and turned her way around the screen. But then the tech exited the room and soon after the doctor came in with some news we weren't ready to receive.

Because we had no health insurance and money was not stable, it was hard for healthcare providers to give me the comprehensive care that I needed. My pregnancy was considered high risk, I didn't have public assistance, and we were paying through the pregnancy in monthly installments. High-risk pregnancies can send families into debilitating debt—and the doctor told us the tests revealed we would be having a baby with special needs. Down syndrome specifically.

I broke down into tears. I was angry with the doctor, who told me to take some time and think about the options. Here I was for the second time around being offered abortion as an option. As I stood in the window to pay for the visit, everyone tried to keep the air light and hopeful.

But I was neither. I just kept my head cupped in my hands and didn't have much to say for the remainder of the visit or the rest of that day. We were to go home and consider all that we had discussed and then call the doctor's office with our decision.

On the way home, we talked about it, asking, "Are we being punished by God?"

We considered our choices carefully. When they first told me, "These are the options that you need to start discussing," I did contemplate having an abortion. I cried the entire fifteen minutes it took to get home. I cried a loud, cleansing, vocal cry. I definitely wanted to know why me. When I walked into the house, my mother was there, working from home. My mother, ever concerned, wanted to talk with me about where I stood. After we finished talking I realized that God would show us how to handle whatever we were faced with. That, if His promises are true, He was going to also give us what we needed to get through this. So that was our decision. I was going to be the mother of a baby with Down syndrome. Now, we needed to figure out what now and what next.

What now was to call the doctor's office and tell them what we decided. I picked up the creamy white receiver from the wall-mounted phone and dialed his office. Now that I was calmer, I could get the rest of my instructions. Next, they scheduled an amniocentesis to learn all we could before she was born.

An amniocentesis test is a prenatal medical procedure performed by withdrawing fluid from the amniotic sac for testing abnormalities and genetic conditions. Because of the risk, procedures like these are usually performed in hospitals as outpatient surgery. But we didn't have money to go to the hospital.

I was afraid, but my doctor wanted to help me. He did have the facilities to perform the procedure at his office, so he decided to offer it in-house. We were only a few blocks from the hospital if we needed to go and this made the test attainable.

The day came for the procedure. His in-office staff prepped everything. I was terrified of the needle he would use and of the pain I might be in, especially outside of the hospital. The staff brought hot wet towels into the room and a surgical platter was wheeled in with all the tools. The doctor assured me I would get through this just fine and began his pre-op routine. He measured and clicked, just like the tech had done before. This time he noticed something new about my baby. He leaped out of the room, promised to be back, and without any other words he left me there in quiet panic.

When he came back several minutes later, he explained that the positioning of my baby would not allow the test to proceed. Her food supply posed an issue with where she was positioned, and the baby was sleeping right at the place he needed to go in with the needle. Several attempts to poke and prod her didn't rouse her. He was afraid that if she moved or jumped, her eye could be taken out by the needle. There were some other clues he found on his examination that day, though, that made him wonder if this baby was older than they had thought. And if so, retesting her results would likely determine her to be outside of the range for concern. The numbers were recalculated and new tests ordered. Quickly, they confirmed that the baby was gestationally further along than we thought and determined that she was, in fact, all right.

Pregnancy will teach patience and the power of prayer. That was probably the first time that I trusted God as an adult. That day, and through that ordeal, I learned God to be Healer, Provider, Burden Sharer, a Way Maker, Miracle Worker, and a Promise Keeper. I decided to trust God instead of believing man. I knew

Recipe Note to Self...

Years ago, as I was building my business, I told God that I wanted to be able to speak intelligently on any subject. I thought it would be valuable to be able to hold an intelligent conversation in any room. I didn't know the magnitude of what I was asking for.

that if I believed God with all my power, that she, being sick, could still be made well.

I didn't know God was going to walk me through so much to give me my own experience to share. I take it back; I changed my mind. There are so many things I don't need to know and don't want to be able to talk about personally.

Both crying and joy are primal universal languages that can be understood cross culturally in any part of the world. My joy is contagious and can strike up a conversation. It can inspire, and it welcomes people to come and fellowship with me. I may not know political figures, breaking news stories, the newest invention, or the hottest investment. However, I do speak a universal language that can be used in any group intelligently. It is unoffensive, multi-lingual, and multicultural. It is the language of understanding.

It is the language of tears and of joy, and for those places that I can't relate, I can show understanding and empathy — and that is a gift I'll take over a myriad of first-hand experiences.

Deep in the Heart of Texas

When I was faced with the challenge of having a baby with special needs, I was angry with the doctor and I was angry with God. When I let go and let God be in control, when I decided that the person this baby would be was marvelous in God's eyes, I began to get excited about the possibilities and the uniqueness of our journey.

It took me having a temper tantrum to get there, but what I've learned through the years is that God understands my tears. I learned that there was an intercessor interpreting the things I couldn't formulate with words (Romans 8:26). Just like a mother knows the cry of her baby and what that baby needs, so does my heavenly Father hear and understand my cries even when I haven't completely formulated what I want. He showed me that if I would trust in Him with all of my heart and not rely on my own wisdom, when I could accept that I didn't know all of the details, that's when He would give me instructions.

He made a way.

God showed me in the toughest times that those who sow in tears will reap in joy. Meaning, if I keep moving, and keep working through my sorrow, God would grant me a harvest that would bring

Recipe Note to Self...

Crying makes it all clear. Tears are like windshield wiper fluid for a car. They clear the view for the driver to see more clearly what is in front of her.

happiness. Weeping may last for a night, but joy is the reward when morning comes. I got those things in my soul and said them until I believed them.

After the tears, I got a clearer vision. I find tears to be just that way, they wash away the cloudiness so that you can see clearly to the decision that makes the most sense, to the decision that needs to be made, for the path that God is working in your favor.

I have had a lot of "Why me?" moments in my life, but I have long since learned to stop posing that question to God. If I ask why me in the bad times, I have to ask why me in the good times too. I learned that in the process of asking why me, I was asking God to take away my burden and give it to somebody else to carry. And I didn't care who had to carry it, I just didn't want it to be me. God showed me that my questioning of Him was selfish. "If not me, then who?" I heard him say, "Should the neighbor get it? Should my co-worker have it? Should my mother bear it?"

God's promises became illuminated for me as I passed through the challenge of motherhood. I can't say that I knew it then; I was too exhausted from being in survival mode to notice. What I did activate was the promise that His grace was sufficient for me and that His strength was made stronger in my weakness (2 Corinthians 12:9). He showed me that as I walked through the water, I wouldn't be overwhelmed because He would be with me (Isaiah 43:2). He wouldn't let me experience trial past my capacity to handle (1 Corinthians 10:13). So, asking that somebody else should take it, someone who God hadn't selected for the task, may be asking for that person to break, to die, to lose their mind. He didn't give it to them because He knew what they could carry. He knew what they already had, even though I couldn't see. Whatever the case, God showed me that the fact that He was presenting me with this was an indication that He would help me get through it.

"Why not me? Who am I to think it shouldn't happen to me?" I have learned to ask instead, "What now?" and "What's next?" I don't even know if I am supposed to ask God, "How?" I know that I am supposed to take the first step, to keep moving forward, and He will show up. That's where the answers were, in asking better questions.

In the case of my pregnancy, the first step was deciding I was going to keep my baby. When I accepted that I would go through with the pregnancy, I took the first step. If I was going to be the mother of a child with Down syndrome, I would accept that and learn how to raise that child. That decision was vital and was not lessened when I found out my child was going to be fine.

A little more than a year after we married, I was twenty years old with four children and a husband. We decided to move our rapidly expanding family to Houston in search of opportunity. The opportunity I got was an introduction to trusting God. It was a new beginning for me mentally and spiritually because I found my faith in God there. I had learned to hear God in New Orleans. In Houston, I learned to listen. Those are two totally separate things. Houston is where I found God.

School of Hard Knocks

As I mentioned earlier, I met François after transferring from Xavier to Holy Cross to pursue a nursing degree. I dropped out after our marriage, but I did not want to abandon my desire for an education that could benefit my family. So while we were living in Houston, I made my way over to Houston Baptist University, a small Christian institution. This marked my first attempt to finish my degree since Holy Cross. I was twenty-one years old, married, and five months pregnant with Brittany. Standing in front of the president's office, while looking over the course offerings, I reflected on my life, feeling as if I had done nothing with my talent or my opportunities.

For some reason, I thought about my eleventh-grade English teacher, who had stirred up a gift in me years earlier. David Boudreaux had come to our class mid-year as a doctoral student from Xavier University. On his first day as our instructor, he said he needed to get to know us and assigned us to write a one-page, introductory paper to assess our writing skills. My paper was a canvas of lies. My real life was too boring to write the truth. So, I told a tale of the day I became a teenage mother, which at that time I was not, and how I lived in the projects, which I did not, and how desperate I was to escape my life, which couldn't have been further from the truth.

Mr. Boudreaux, genuinely concerned, approached me after class to tell me services were available to help me, and he wanted to make sure I got help. When I responded, "Oh, yeah, that. It was all a lie."

Then I chuckled. That was about the most tyrannical thing I have ever done. He wasn't upset, but he asked me what I wanted to be.

"A doctor," I said with conviction. "I'm going to help people and heal the world."

"You're a writer," he said. He introduced me to a new option—that writers could be journalists who write for newspapers and magazines or anchor the evening news. That spoke to a desire I had never uttered in public—that I knew one day I would be famous. I wasn't sure what for, but I wanted to be a star. I firmly believed that God wouldn't waste this fabulous name on me if no one was ever to know it. So, I had a job to do—to become memorable. I remembered wanting to sit behind the desk as a television anchor. I had watched Hoda Kotb every day and Sally-Ann Roberts, a co-anchor on WWL-TV in New Orleans. She is the older sister of Robin Roberts, co-anchor of ABC's *Good Morning America*. Their reflections showed me that girls like me could become women like them.

My journey to becoming a woman like Hoda, Sally-Ann, or Robin wasn't a quick one. It would take two more years before I was able to fully devote myself to finishing my degree. The first time I enrolled at Houston Baptist, I was only able to take a class here and there because of the demands of taking care of my family and helping to support our household in the ways that I could.

The second time I enrolled at Houston Baptist University came only after a number of life disruptions, including our family moving back to New Orleans and then back to Houston again. It was only after my husband was injured on the job that I was able to devote my time to finishing my undergraduate degree. I had given up my job at BellSouth to take care of my husband, but it gave me time to go back to school.

Now at the Houston Baptist University admissions office for the second time around, paper application in hand and hundreds of miles away from my mom, I was afraid to declare what I wanted to be on paper for fear she would say there was no future in journalism either. Then I thought, "Heck, I am somebody's wife and mom, and I'm scared of what my mother would say about this?" I pumped myself up to declare a major: mass media with a concentration in journalism and photography.

In eighteen months, I chewed up that program, determined to rewrite my life's story, and I graduated with distinction in an area to which I could apply myself. However, after graduation, no matter how much I applied for jobs, the only thing I was successful at landing was my job as household manager, wife, and mother of five.

There I was in Houston, away from family and friends in New Orleans, and our phone was usually disconnected. When it wasn't, I would call my mom and friends back home and talk for hours. After peak hours, the phone rates were cheaper, but I had no discipline to wait. I would often run our phone bill up so high we couldn't afford to pay it.

Because of the phone situation, I wrote a lot of letters in the late 90s. I did my best to imagine it as an adventure. I even managed to find some old childhood friendships and make pen pal connections. Those didn't last long. We didn't have much in common anymore except an interest in where the other had landed. I had a husband nearly eleven years my senior and a ready-made family we had started building upon a year after we were married.

We had no other family in the area. I didn't know anyone where we lived. We had made connections with families at a church, but it was so far away from our apartment that we often couldn't go for lack of gas to get there, or my husband would be at work with the sole family car. I often felt secluded and would make deals with God saying, "God, if you let me get the phone back on, I promise not to ever run it up that high again."

Having no dial tone was such a prominent recurring theme in my life that my mom set up a Morse Code sort of pattern that I could use to call home for free. For long-distance calls, customers were not charged unless the other party answered. When I needed to talk, I could call home on the pay phone behind the apartment office at the complex where I lived, let the phone ring twice, and hang up. They would know it was me calling and call me back. I would have to collect enough quarters to make the call, all while hoping someone who didn't know our system wouldn't answer my mother's phone and make me lose my coins. If no one answered, the pay phone would return all my coins. If my prayers were answered, the phone would ring back shortly, and I would hear my mother's loving voice so full of joy that she also could hear that we were well on the other end of the polished black phone receiver. The saddest were times I didn't even have enough coins to make her phone ring.

Collecting coins would sometimes become a mass operation. I taught my children to help me find enough coins in the house to make a call. Barney, the purple dinosaur on television, taught my youngest children the joy of cleaning to music. All Barney had to say was "Clean up," and let the music begin. We would lift all the cushions, putting our fingers in the crevices of the sofa. Tiny hands can reach farther, so Popsicles and a trip to the pay phone were a reward for them and for me if we could gather enough coins.

In those days you could also call collect, meaning the other party would pay once the operator asked them to consent. I would call my mother collect. An operator would ask me to say my name so that she could announce me to the person answering. When the operator asked her if she would accept, she would decline the call and ring the number at the pay phone. Sometimes when the line would open I had just enough time to tell my mom I was in distress and that I needed her to accept the charges. In those times she would do that.

Other times my mom would send letters and include a calling card inside that I could use to call home. Those calling cards were like a gift of fresh air, a chance for me to breathe and have a lifeline back home.

Standing in the elements, whether cold, raining, breezy, or warm, to make a call, it was always bitter out there. It was limiting, limited time I could talk to my mom or my friends, limited money to spend to make much-needed human connections. I wanted something different.

My husband worked his share of twelve-hour shifts to make overtime pay and slept most of the day to be on to the next shift. My babies were small then and watched a lot of *Sesame Street*, *Teletubbies*, *Barney & Friends*, and all kinds of other PBS shows. I had a system in those days, and quiet time for me was always scheduled around watching Oprah. It was one of the only things I felt I had true control over in my life, nap time and watching her television show.

On the rare occasions when my mom could visit, I would soak up all the cooking and conversation she had to offer. Sitting there in the living room on my striped Kelly green-and-tan sofa, she listened until her ears bled. I must have been talking about the kids' television shows when my mom hit my proverbial pause button and said, "Mignon, is there anything that you can talk about besides children's television?"

Embarrassed, I confessed, "That's all I have, and it's all I know."

I could feel her body language anguishing. Indeed, she was happy to be spending time with her daughter and grandchildren, but in the moments that followed her observation, I know she wished to swallow those words back into her face and send them right back to the belly where she had cooked them up before spitting them out.

Silence tastes salty when words are hurtful, but at the same time necessary—for both of us. It was necessary that she know what my existence had really been and necessary for me to realize that even though she was glad to be there, she had not come to Nashville to hear stories about Big Bird. I babbled too much about things that didn't matter much to her.

For me, I was indulging the privilege of talking to someone who could respond, and I hadn't found much worth saying to someone who wasn't stuck in the time trap that was my current life. As painful as it was to hear her assessment of me, it made me realize that I'd better start looking for something valuable to add to me, apart from my role as a mother or a wife. My car, at that time a Toyota Camry, had recently been repossessed in what would be one of several similar experiences in my life that would teach me about finances and living within my means. Waking up to find my car had been taken felt like robbery. It was robbery, minus the broken glass. My neighbor had knocked on the door late in the midnight hour asking if I was okay. Coming home late, he saw my car being towed from the complex and wanted to make sure everything was all right.

Not long before, an industrial trailer full of tools had been stolen from the complex. Nobody saw or heard a thing, but we were determined never to allow that to happen to us again, so neighbors were on the lookout for anything that seemed strange.

I called the apartment office asking if the complex had cameras, so I could see who had taken my car. Unlike me, the office assistant was not convinced my car was stolen. In her very condescending voice, the office clerk asked if my car had been towed on the bank's behalf. "Why would they do that, Ma'am?" I asked naively.

It seemed like no one cared about my car being stolen. I pleaded my case to deaf ears. Maybe the clerk thought she knew "my type," but I knew I didn't want to be categorized.

Recipe Note to My Younger Self...

"You may be able to catch bees with honey, but you can sure attract and keep them with bright flowers."

I had spoken with someone at the bank, made payment arrangements, and paid what I could on the past due balance. I learned that it matters not that you've "made arrangements." When the bank grows impatient with your inability to pay, they will pick up your car, without warning, in the middle of the night, with your children's car seats and whatever else you love inside.

I wept. I sobbed. I beat the table and demanded that they return my car. "Don't you care that I have children?"

"Obviously, you don't care, Mrs. François," the words came lashing back at me across the phone.

No sympathy. No understanding. I became angry. Insulting. Demanding. My rudeness returned a resolve on the other end that this conversation was over. I could retrieve my things at the address she provided without hesitation. She only paused so that I could get a pencil to write. That was as much kindness as she had to muster for my case.

Here's where I hear my mother saying, "You can catch more bees with honey." Clearly, you can't catch bees once the nectar has been sucked out of its hive. I slammed the phone repeatedly, clinching my fists and screaming in a fit of rage. I had given them my money, and now I had nothing to show for it. I felt helpless and sorry for myself. No one else shared that sentiment of sorrow for my life.

I tried to get it back, but I couldn't catch up the payments.

I was forced to drive Nellie. I refer to the car as a person because she was like the other woman that had my husband's heart and attention. Though she would prove not to be the only one vying for that position, she made my life the most living kind of hell. That car hated me. If it was going to break down, it was going to break down with me in it.

My husband loved Nellie. And as much as he loved her, I hated her and was hated by her with equal fervor and intensity. That thing was so big it glided down the street, floated even, like a boat on the water. Nellie had an olive coat of paint and a white "rag top" that had long since passed its heyday. Loose pieces of the top flapped in the air as age had loosened its grip around the seals. François was proud of Nellie, too, but I never quite understood why he chose to drive that over something more modern. Nellie was a tank, though I'm really not sure whether her passengers ever truly needed protection. Nevertheless, God bless the child who might collide with her.

The driver's seat was completely worn from use. The foam seat cushions pressed their way toward the light through holes where the leather had worn completely through. The back seats, on the other hand, were pristine, likely because they hadn't held many passengers over Nellie's lifetime. She boasted a stereophonic Hi-Fi sound and had a radio with a detachable face to prevent it from being stolen. Nellie was a true gas guzzler that sucked up all our extra money, especially with the tinkering needed to keep her running. Despite how we invested in her, Nellie left me stranded at every chance possible.

Like that day I needed to go to the store. I dropped François off at the Southern Pacific Railroad yard where he worked as an electrician. The dusty, unpaved railyard with its train cars scattered about looked more like a manicured junkyard. It was in the heart of the city of Houston, so the commute was far and took a lot of gas due to Nellie's eight-cylinder engine. Putting gas in the car was painful, not just for the price, but also getting to the gas tank, which was hidden behind the license plate. The hinged license plate had to be pulled down like a secret door. It reminded me of Murphy beds that pull down from the wall to reveal a sleeping place on the other side. Once the license plate was pulled down, it revealed a metal gas cap with a lock. It required inserting the special gas cap key, and my experiences with Nellie and her keys were consequential.

Later that night, after shopping for groceries, I approached the car in prayer. "God, let this key work, please. Please, God!" I threw in one more, "Please, God!" for good measure and put the key in the lock to get my children secured inside. I pushed, I jiggled, I jostled, and I wiggled the key. I prayed some more. The lock would not be moved. I wrestled with that key for nearly a half hour. My middle finger was beginning to bruise and swell from my constant wrestling with that key. Tears began to well up in my eyes as I tried to figure out what to do next. I couldn't call a cab. I didn't have the money for that. Calling my husband was out of the question because I had the car. How would he get to me?

I wanted to abandon that car right there in the Fiesta grocery store parking lot. I imagined myself carrying the groceries home and walking with the children the several blocks to our apartment. The more I worked through my mental calculations, the risk outweighed the reward. The FM 1960 Road was an extremely busy highway with four lanes in each direction. Even with a stoplight at the intersection, I would never have enough time to cross eight lanes with a toddler, two children, and the groceries we had gotten from the store.

I felt abandoned. In a moment of defeat, I gathered myself, my groceries, and my children and went inside to call my husband to find a way to come help. It took about another hour, but he showed up with a coworker driving a railroad truck they used for chasing trains along the rails.

Outside of the Fiesta grocery store were vendors who roasted corn on the cob that they spiced with lime and chili seasonings. I bought my children a treat of Mexican corn, and I watched them enjoy eating as they sat on the curb. Alexius, our happy little third grader, and his trusty little sidekick, baby brother Dillon, knew nothing of the turmoil I felt as baby girl Brittany grew hungry waiting for their dad to arrive. Those bottles under my shirt were about to come in handy once again. Thank God for breastmilk to the rescue. I had to nurse her on the curb. The whole ordeal was embarrassing for me to say the least.

Sitting on the side of the sidewalk, I felt helpless. My pleated denim skort and polo shirt were not much for warding off mosquitoes, and my clothes had begun to stick to my sweaty, uncomfortable skin as the sun disappeared into the moonlit night. Sadness welled up like hot embers in my eyes along with an unwillingness to keep experiencing this pain.

Finally, their dad pulled up like that superhero, Mr. Incredible, but I knew this was not supposed to be my life. He popped the key in the lock, and it moved like churned butter. He offered to take us home and drive himself back to work so that I could avoid another ordeal in the middle of the night when it would be time to pack up our babies and fetch him from work. I accepted.

I still have a callous from turning Nellie's ignition key in those days—third finger, right hand.

When I think back on Nellie and all the memories that were made within her frame, I laugh sometimes. My children mostly have fond recollections. Dillon remembers riding in the front seat on game day when he was the star starting player on the basketball team. He had a theme song as they arrived, Dr. Dre's 2001 album blaring "The Next Episode." Alex's fondest memory focused mostly on a secret that only he and Nellie held—a half-moon drawn in between two screws on the back seat footrest that formed a smiley face. Lauren remembers mostly counting all the things she could discover through the rusted hole in the floorboard as we traveled along the highway. We laughed as we reminisced on why her feet never touched the ground on any of those adventures. Funny that my children recall fondly the things that are daggers to my soul. Maybe that's why the Bible tells us we should become like children. The viewpoint from their place in the world is always looking upward.

I believe that nothing just happens to you—everything that's happening is for you. In the Bible, the Apostle Paul says, "And we know that all things work together for good to them that love God, to them who are the called according to his purpose" (Romans 8:28, KJV). To me, the word "all" means everything, not some things, not just some times. That means no matter what, it's always working out for you. So, nothing is happening to you. It's happening for you if all things are working for your good.

Later, after I got a job, my mom brought me her car, and let me take over the note on it. It was a gold 1996 Nissan Altima. Then, after my husband got a settlement from an accident at work, he bought me a brand-new car right off the Volvo showroom floor.

I have been processing a lot of those memories. One of the things I feel God has recently urged me to do is go back and visit places where I have experienced major hurt and create a new memory there so that those places can't hurt me anymore.

I think that's what all my experiences used to feel like—like I was being degraded by the people who were looking on and telling me that I wasn't good enough. Those were the experiences I never needed to go back to. I needed to be able to make it on my own, even if it meant we were going to eat red beans every day. If we had to that's what we were going to do. I think that those are the things that sharpened my ability to say, "I'm going to find something that I can do to help us win."

In obedience, I took a pilgrimage to Houston. That visit was the start of me fleshing out my adult story. I believe Houston is where I started becoming Mignon.

A Gift from My Parents

*"You have to do your due diligence
to make your name great."*

Nothing exists apart from words. In fact, in the beginning was the word, the word was with God and the word was God (John 1:1). I am the product of words that my dad said to my mom that she liked.

Our names are words with meaning and synonyms meant to describe and adeptly identify who we are and how we show up in the world. I knew I would be famous someday. I always knew it. I

Recipe Note to Self...

"Your name follows you wherever you go,
but it's your reputation that always
shows up first."

Catherine Moody

just didn't know why—not because I am overly talented or gifted but because I knew that God wouldn't waste a fabulous name like Mignon Theriot on a person nobody was ever going to know. In fact, I decided partly that my husband was the one for me because his name fit so perfectly with my famous name. It couldn't have been better orchestrated unless I had been born exactly with that name.

"You have to do your due diligence to make your name great," I told myself.

My name is the wonderful gift that my parents gave me on the day I was born. It was their intention that when I walked into a room people would unmistakably know who I am. Though I had a long and vigorous history of hating my name, mainly during my childhood and teen years, I grew to love what it represented.

When I was young, my name haunted me. On the first day of school, when the teacher called out everyone else's name, she had a cadence to her roll call. But then there would be the inevitable slow, unexpected pause that would always signal the beginning of an awkward moment. Over the years I learned to slump down in my seat and slowly raise my hand, cringing at the sound of my name being butchered.

"Do you really think that's someone's name?" I'd be thinking. It is pronounced Meen-'yȯn Tear-RIO. After I started attending more diverse schools that didn't happen as much. The teachers knew how to pronounce my name or at least they knew to practice it before they called it out loud.

As I grew older, still, I began to realize something special— when I introduced myself, people would take notice. They would practice it, ask me to repeat it, make small talk about it, and even give me a history lesson about my name. I have had my share of conversations about my name. All these decades later, I receive with gladness what my momma gave me. So, the first life lesson I learned in legacy building: there is power in a name.

As I grew older, I began to recognize that God was trying to show me I needed to have an authentic experience with Him. "I need you to show up in the world the way I made you unapologetically, Mignon, and I need you to understand that your name is unique and different on purpose, that I whispered that name to your mother and told her to call you that, so that when you walked into a room, people wouldn't be confused that 'Yeah, I'm talking about her.'

On the day I was born, my parents gave me a name, a name I am certain they changed many times before landing on the one I carry. They wanted me to know who I was. On the day I was born my parents also gave me their family name, Theriot. They wanted me to know whose I was. And then finally, on the day I was born, my heavenly father gave me His name so that I would know that He would be with me wherever I go. What is His name? I Am. How do I know that?

I have had my share of conversations about my name. One conversation I cherish most was one I had with Dr. Pat Jackson, a spiritual therapist who taught me a new perspective on my name that would forever change how I felt about it being who *I am*. All these decades later, I receive with gladness what my momma gave me: there is power in a name.

In Exodus 3, we read about Moses talking to God at a burning bush. During their conversation, God instructs Moses that he was being sent to Pharaoh to lead His people, the Israelites, out of Egypt. Moses protested and asked what he should tell the people if they asked the name of the one that had sent him. God replied to Moses.

"I AM WHO I AM. This is what you are to say to the Israelites: 'I AM has sent me to you'" (Exodus 3:14, NIV).

The Bible says if you lay your bed in hell, I AM is there (see Psalm 139:3). I can't even introduce myself without saying His name. He wanted me to know that no matter where I go the I AM is there. I AM is with you. So that when I walk in a room and say, "I am Mignon François," it is a reminder that the great I AM is with me always, even into the end of the world. It is a consistent reminder that when I walk in the door, the I AM goes before me. *I am Mignon* is a sentence sealed in beauty by my heavenly father.

Best of all, the I AM makes all things possible. In fact, impossible becomes "I am possible" when the I AM gets inserted.

What I love about the naming process is this: the Bible says that there is nothing new under the sun (Ecclesiastes 1:9). If we accept that as truth, then the way that names are doled out must also be ancient. In Scripture, some expectant parents would get a visit from God or an angel to announce what the parents should name their new baby. Babies were named based on what their personalities would be or how the person would show up in the world. If that was the case years before, and if our John 1 reference is correct, we are still being named the same way. The difference between then and now is that we have become so far removed from God, we often can't hear him speak distinctly.

I firmly believe and maintain today that either we will live out the meaning of our name or the adversary set up against it will win when we do not know what our name says about us.

My name is Mignon. A search on the etymology of my name returned many words synonymous with my name. It means: lover, darling, dainty, pleasing, gentle, kind, friendship, affection, memory, affectionate thought, caring—all things that resonate within my personality.

"Favorite" is another meaning of my name. It didn't dawn on me until this discovery that I had struggled my entire life with middle child syndrome, never being anyone's favorite and never imagining myself as being good enough. In my adulthood, I learned that I was favorited or favored by God and knowing that was a game changer. My name even shared a life lesson as I considered that steaks are called filet mignon. And why so? Because mignon is the choice cut of meat that delivers the most succulent part of the steak. It has to be cut away. Cut! I was cut many times by circumstances but have emerged more loving, more affectionate, and more kind, looking always for the lesson, for joy, and for forgiveness. If it wasn't for the cuts, I wouldn't be the woman I am.

When I discovered that God intended for me to exist in the world as a human representation of all these beautiful words, my mission became clear: to spread nurturing joy. Let me offer an example of what I mean. Take the words "gift card."

While cleaning a new vehicle my daughter acquired, she came across an object that had gotten wedged in the vacuum. Thinking she might have sucked up one of her children's toys, she dismantled the hose to fish out the object. What she discovered was a dirty gift card that looked like it had been in the car for a very long time. At first thought, she decided to discard the piece of plastic that seemed too worn to be of value. But after a second thought, she reasoned the possibility that the card might actually have value. She decided to pursue the second thought and presented the gift card at her favorite family restaurant. To her surprise, the gift card had ten dollars on it, enough to buy a meal. In her hands, the gift card, which she could have perceived as worthless, would have been misused. The money, the treasure it held, would have gone to waste. Instead, she decided to explore what she knew about gift cards and their potential. She decided to activate an opportunity to believe. What could happen if I only believed?

Gift cards have loaded potential that can be used completely or wasted completely. Had she not known what gift cards could do, had she not known what it means to possess a gift card, she would have dismissed it as trash clogging up her vacuum. That same gift card in a child's hands or another person who did not believe would be dismissed as a dirty piece of plastic.

I am submitting that this is the power essentially in knowing the meaning of our names. They are loaded with potential. If we don't know who we are called to be, or the purpose that God planted within us, we might become misused, our talents misappropriated, or our ideas mismanaged. A person who knows their name means one to be treasured is not easily letting themselves be discounted.

I believe firmly that we will close our eyes in forever sleep for one of two reasons: either we fulfilled our purpose or we ignored it. Finding purpose began when I learned the meaning of my name and what God called me to be. Before that, I was tricked into thinking something less.

And I definitely did not think I was "beautiful." That's what the word Mignon means in French. When my mother sat with God to consider her child, He had said something poignant about what and who that child would be. Imagine knowing that your name is a representation of what God thought of you and that He would tell your mother that the baby she was carrying would be beautiful.

I hardly thought of myself as beautiful, though. No one ever clamored for my attention—from grade school to graduation. On the rare occasions when it did happen, I became enamored. I quickly fell in love with those who proved not to love me in return. The adversary led me to believe that I was ugly—my nose was too big, lips too large, eyes too strange—as early as eight years old. But one day, when I was thirty-three years old, I saw a picture of myself, an undeniably beautiful photo of me. It was then that I discovered my true appearance, and I gained confidence. As I grew in self-assurance, I began to believe that I was smart enough to create ideas that people would follow, and businesses began to birth from me.

So until I was in my early thirties, I maintained that I couldn't see beauty, at least not on me. Ugly is all I saw. Maybe ugly is too harsh; maybe it was mostly awkward. I was the victim of being the child my father didn't love—and digging a bit deeper, did he even like me? I never asked. Maybe I was too afraid to ever really know the truth.

Obedient Hair

So, I was an awkward girl named Beautiful. My nose was so big, and it has a hook on the end that could be grabbed. I had a "five head" not a forehead. My clothes were all wrong, and I never felt like I fit in. My eyes were hazel, not even quite green, but barely brown, almost a muddied, dirty shade of olive.

My sandy-brown hair kissed often by the sun was burnished blondish with highlighted strands of gold and amber. The coils that matted at the base of my neck were the source of my tears with every attempt to brush it as I winced and jumped. My hair never slicked neatly around my hairline to plaster swirly smooth edges of "baby hair" bangs like the other Black girls' did. My hair, straightened by relaxers since the age of five, was always loose and fly-away with an unkempt appearance even moments after being combed.

Second grade recess—that's the first time I got confirmation I wasn't pretty. The bell rang and all the kids bolted outside. We were all gathered on the sidewalk where the girls had been talking about the two boys in our second-grade class that all the girls thought were so cute. One of them was already spoken for by one of the pretty girls in our group, but Mikey was up for grabs. Mikey was a brown-haired White boy with a bowl-style haircut and sharp, straight bangs. I remember his teeth. They were crooked but not fighting for space as he had a large gap between the two in front. His cheeks were stained rosy red, and his skin had a pale, milky skin tone. He was adorable to me and all the other girls in the second grade. I used to dream about marrying Mikey but felt I could never say that aloud because he was white. Still, that did not stop me from dreaming that he would be my husband someday. Dreams are free.

All the girls gathered on the sidewalk when Mikey came over. Cherri had decided that he liked her, and Mikey decided that chasing her was the way to prove it. As the game of tag ensued, one of the girls tagged Mikey and jetted off into the field. Mikey quickly went after her. In fact, as each one tagged him, a chasing pursued. By now, Mikey was trying to catch all the other girls. All except one — me.

I chased, and I tagged. I ran, and I chased. "You can't catch me," I taunted. Mikey turned and ran in the opposite direction. I was right there and the easiest target. Yelling his name and thrusting myself about in my solo game of tag, I tried to get him to catch me. Mikey stopped. He looked at me. His face was bewildered, tinted with a little disgust and confusion. "I'm not chasing you," he said, whipping his hair around. "I don't even like you."

His words cut like a dagger to my heart. I was one of the only Black girls in my class, one of the few in our entire school, in fact. Of course, he didn't like me, I was Black, and to him, I was ugly. Devastated and conquered, I gave up.

Does "humiliated" have a sound? No, it's too scared to have a voice. Humiliated is silent.

Humiliated does, however, have an appearance, a style even. Her shoulders drape like saggy curtains hanging on her body as if she doesn't wear her own clothes; but rather, her clothes wear her. Her eyes cast a downward gaze so that the beholder will never look upon her directly to see who she really is and where she might be going.

Feeling utterly defeated, I walked over to the steps that led to the basement of the Aurora Seventh-day Adventist Church, where our school was housed. The short stack of gray concrete steps became my sanctuary as I awaited the end of recess and my embarrassment. As I plopped down to sit, Humiliation wrapped her arms around me and confirmed what I already suspected—I was ugly.

After that degrading experience, I struggled for years thereafter to define myself as beautiful. Though I must say that I have recognized beautiful features about myself, when you put them all together, they seemed to me to be a mishmash of awkwardness. I guess since I never counted it much when someone else did see value; I simply did not believe them. I would never have the worth, the rhyme and reason, to fall in love.

My sandy blonde hair was never curly enough, straight enough, tamed enough, or wild enough. I begged my mother on a regular basis to allow me to color it, but she always inevitably said no.

"Do you know what women pay for the highlights you naturally have?" she would say.

Since I have come to appreciate the struggle of other women to obtain the just right ratio of blonde-to-red highlights, I decided to be satisfied. Even though I'd really love to dye it fuchsia, I'll never dare. Mom told me that even once I dyed my hair, it would never be enough.

I just wanted more than anything to have good hair.

"All hair is good, Mignon. If it's on top of your head, that's good. Be grateful," she would say.

I think mostly I believed that she believed in what she was saying because she had billowing curls that transformed into smooth, shiny, silk under the heat of a curling iron. It blew in the wind with careless abandon and fell back into place with a run through from her fingers. It was not the kind that called your neck to twist and contort just at being tamed by a brush.

I learned to appreciate the thick, coarse, tender-headed mass that is mine to own. I would just rather call it obedient. If I lay down, it mashes. And it will stay firmly planted until I wrangle it back in place.

Like other mental and emotional spaces, I am recognizing in my life, the more I pay attention to it and give it a regimen, the more it will show up the way I want. It is like training a dog. You must be consistent. It hardly ever breaks, rarely splits, something I cannot confidently say of all of the other relationships I have had misunderstandings with.

Grandma's Hands

Ethel Paul Theriot Brown was the mother of nine children, my father being the seventh child. For reasons I won't understand in this lifetime, he was separated from her before he was school age and was not reunited with her until he came home on leave from the US Air Force.

I have fond memories of her. Every time we came to visit, she was happy to see us, though her face did not always indicate her joy. Her look was stoic—she was serious, and a woman who enjoyed high quality. It seems that we always found her in the kitchen in the midst of making something. Whenever I would come into her house, she would always say, "Bring those fine legs over here so I can look at my legs." She thought that I was fine and would make it her business to affirm that aloud. I knew that my body shape came from her, and I knew that she thought that I was beautiful. To her, I was a walking reminder of her youth.

To look at my sister Alaina would be to get a glimpse of my grandmother's younger face, which is a female replica of my father's. Recognizing them as family is an easy task, especially knowing their name Theriot. So it's not a far-fetched surprise that a stranger could happen upon my father, become aware of his last name, and know whose he was. Theirs is a strong genome.

When she died, I hadn't laid eyes on her in probably eighteen years. I couldn't face that disappointed look. I knew nobody expected me to have a baby, but the reality was, I was living a truth that wasn't going to change.

Saturdays after church, I could pass right in front of her house on the way home and not stop. On our last visit, I had stopped by to introduce my baby, who by then had his first pair of hard-soled shoes and was beginning to walk. She told me not to be a stranger and that she would be on the lookout for things he needed. But I did become estranged and never made it back before Hurricane Katrina decimated her home and took her to live outside of the city in her last years.

Standing at my grandmother's casket, I saw something in her that I alone, of all her grandchildren my parents bore, possessed. My whole life growing up, I thought that I had my father's hands, and I hated them. "These are big manly hands. I hate these hands," I said often wishing for something more feminine like those of my younger sisters. On the day that we said goodbye to my grandmother, I looked down at her lying in the casket and realized my hands are just like hers. I have short fat fingers. Most women have dainty fingers but not me. My ring size when I got married was nine and a half. Even after I lost weight, my ring size stopped at eight and a half. That's the smallest my ring finger size had ever been.

These manly hands that I have, which my sisters take great delight in teasing me about, were not those of a man, but rather those belonging to a woman who held an entire lineage, a legacy. These hands were an identifiable characteristic of the Paul family, my grandmother's heritage. The fact that I had been given them made me wonder, What if God had done this all for me? What if he had placed the responsibility to carry this legacy in these hands? Could that be the reason why my father had them too? The reason that he would be sent away to live with strangers and stay there until adulthood, that his newfound family would be connected to his little girl who also bore those hands, that the lady who loved him would also love her and place a gift in her young hands that only she would be able to carry, a gift so great that it could only be placed into trusted, sturdy hands?

Could it be the possible reason God had given me the ability to build something for our family was in these hands? He knew I would take what was given, use it, and then share it using these very hands.

When I look down at my hands, I can always see that these are Grandma's hands and feel connected to her.

Finding My Beauty

Long before photo filters and Instagram were available to anyone with a phone, a photoshoot finally revealed to me my own beauty.

I pulled up to the house with a lump in my throat. Of the many photoshoots I had been on in my life, none had ever seemed so nerve-racking as this. I climbed out of the car and slammed the door hard. It screeched and moaned so loud. Even the neighbors knew I had arrived. My stupid car! Just when I had decided to crawl back inside and drive off pretending that I never made it. I mean, I could have blamed anything on that car. My host, Karima, appeared behind her storm door. My friend bounded out of the house so happy I had taken her up on her offer to take pictures of me that day. Her beautiful brunette mane framed her face as she leaned in for a hug hello. I was a photographer at the time, and she had suggested the shoot. She said that I always made everybody else feel beautiful and she wanted me to feel that too.

"Let me help you with your stuff," she said, eager to get me going.

Embarrassed, I unlocked the trunk only to reveal the most pitiful rags that I called my Saturday night best. The tops hardly matched the bottoms that seemed even more pathetic as she held them out. Stylish is her middle name. It doesn't matter where she finds it. This lady can turn thrift store bargains into treasures.

She picked up my outfits, grabbed all that she could handle, and beckoned me along. We ran inside to get started like we did when we were ten-year-old schoolgirls.

Once inside, with everything all sprawled out, I was hesitant.

"Show me what you've got," she said.

I held out a white t-shirt with cap sleeves. I smiled, "It's my favorite."

I hadn't noticed that grease stain on it before now. Never once acknowledging the stain, she snatched the shirt from my hand.

"Next!" she said, waving her hands as if to say bring it on or move it along.

I presented my brown suede, wedge boots proudly. With a coupon, I had gotten these $78 specials for a mere twenty bucks.

She looked thoughtfully. I could sense her wheels spinning. "What the heck am I going to do with this?" is what she must have been thinking.

"C'mon," she said, motioning for me to follow her into the next room. There, as I started to release my thoughts and let the whiz perform her magic, she sat me down and plucked and prodded at my eyebrows, tussled my freshly shampooed hair, and painted a face upon mine as if it were a fresh blank canvas. A few pieces from her closet added to my wretched little worn-out fragments that I called clothes, and "Bam!" beauty emerged from the rubbish. After a few hours, and an immeasurable magnitude of flashes, it happened.

I saw her.

She was beautiful, gorgeous, breathtaking. She was staring back at me in a photograph, and I couldn't deny that I knew her. "She" was me. No filters, just facts. I couldn't say my nose was too big, or my forehead too large. I could not claim that my smile was wrong, or that the look on my face was weird. From this angle, all I could see was pretty.

At thirty-two years old, it happened. I became beautiful for the very first time. I had lived my life as this ugly girl, at least in my head. I couldn't deny that the person in this picture was beautiful to me. It was the first time I saw myself as pretty. It was undeniable that the girl in that picture was beautiful, and that girl was me. Imagine, all that time I spent in arrogance, elevating my opinion above God's.

Before now, I had always had a playful personality that I kept under quiet wraps. When I walked into a room, I wanted so badly to unleash the girl I knew I could be and own the room. But the fear that gripped me made me believe I couldn't.

Instantly, literally with a camera's flash, the dismissive looks became stares, at least inside my head, not because I was awkward but because something about me was unusual. Nothing about me, except my perspective, had actually changed. Funny that "awkward" and "unusual" are synonyms that, when chosen carefully, cause the whole scene to change. That little, tiny shift, that tiny tweak in my mindset gave me the confidence to let the world see my light.

Recipe Note to Self...

Two are better than one, because they have a good return for their labor: If either of them falls down, one can help the other up. Keep friends around you who will use their iron to sharpen yours (Proverbs 27:17) seeking nothing in return except that you would be fly.

A Baby Bump in the Road

nearly fell out on the floor when I realized what was going on with me. Brittany was in school and loving it, and I was settling into mornings at my desk. Less than a year had passed and we had moved into a beautiful split-level home that I loved despite the long commute to work every day. I really liked my workplace and I had gained a great sense of fulfillment and confidence from my contributions at work.

Besides this little headache...hmmm.

I had been having a little headache every day. I asked myself whether I was particularly tired, had I skimped on drinking enough water, or maybe I was hungry. There was a really good dining facility downstairs, but it was not quite lunch.

I thought a little more about the headaches I was having and couldn't seem to get rid of. A thought pounded its way to the forefront of my mind and I yanked out the calendar at my desk. "Am I late? Why haven't I had my period? Or did I have a period, already?" Keeping up with that kind of thing was never really my jam, and with each new pregnancy, I clearly hadn't figured out how this worked anyway. And frankly, to this day I don't know what

135

captured my attention on that particular day to cause me to begin contemplating the possibility of pregnancy in the first place — except maybe that things were going so well at the time.

On the way home, I got a pregnancy test and took it into the bathroom. Two bright blue lines appeared in the results window, and rather quickly I might add.

Pregnant? No, wait! Is it one line or two? Let me do that again.

I tore open the second test from the package and peed on the stick. This time I made sure to do it the way they tell you in the doctor's office — careful not to get something foreign on the stick, like bacteria, that could cause a false result. I let a little pee trickle out into the toilet and then full-on soaked that puppy under a warm steady stream. Those pesky blue lines showed up again — in sync behind the tiny plastic viewer. I began slowly reading over the box instructions — once, and then again, the second time making sure I completely understood the result.

Two lines. Pregnant.

That's when I actually did it. My knees gave way and I just dropped. Getting up, scratch that, peeling myself off the floor, I was crying and questioning "Why me?"

I was twenty-seven years old with a great career and pregnant. "Not now...things are just getting on track in my life.

I had been at Home Depot for one year when I found out I was pregnant, again, with what would be our sixth child, five and half years after the last one.

Working at Home Depot had made me feel like the drama in my life was finally over. My youngest child was off to school, and I had a job that I really enjoyed after having applied for so many. Finally, I was going to get my freedom!

I cried a lot. I didn't want to be pregnant again. I didn't want to go back to feedings and formula and, most of all, I didn't want to give up the life I was beginning to love. More than not wanting a baby, I was distraught at being thrown off my successful career path.

When I gave birth to Xavier in 2001, I knew that I was going to have to quit working at Home Depot. After the bad experiences I had with the mistreatment of my son Dillon in daycare back in Houston, I vowed I would never have another baby of mine unprotected in the care of strangers, at least until they were old enough to communicate if something was wrong. Not ever!

I was equipped with a good support system for the baby; my oldest children were in high school and my youngest were five and eight when Xavier was born in 2001. I gave birth to him on August 22, twenty days before the World Trade Center terrorist attacks on September 11. As the morning of 9/11 pushed its way through the slats of our closed master bedroom blinds, all of that changed. I heard a desperate plea that woke me from our first good rest as a nursing mom and newborn duo.

I thought it was another one of those almost too real night terrors I described earlier. This, however, was the daytime. Having been up earlier nursing my newborn baby, who was the size of a ten-pound sack of potatoes, I was struggling to wake up from the space between "Is this a dream or is this reality." Listening to the news as Diane Sawyer desperately reported, in my half-asleep mode, I vividly saw the world in a panic and believed the Second Coming of Christ or the apocalypse was actively happening. It was as if the ABC special report had interrupted my regularly scheduled dream to bring this breaking news.

When I finally came to, I still thought it was the apocalypse and Jesus himself might crack the sky for all of us to see on *Good Morning America*.

The words of Revelation 1:7, "And every eye shall see him," was all I could think about in those moments.

I swooped up my sleeping baby and cradled him close just as his father came through the door for a routine mommy-and-me check in.

Have you seen the news?" he asked.

"Yes! Please go get my children," I said, stiffened by the prospects that lay in the unknown.

From elementary to high school, he collected them. If Jesus was going to come today, I wanted to meet him with my family all in one place. While it was not the Second Coming, the day reiterated the value of my family and fortified my desire to keep them close.

I did try to go back to work after Xavier's birth, and the team of associates I worked with made it easy to give working a try. Home Depot's management established a lactation station in the building for moms like me, and my boss and coworkers made it easy to transition with him. They even gifted me a top-of-the-line Medela breast pump, complete with the coolest carrying case that looked just like a messenger bag.

Recipe Side Note...

God cares that you hate traffic and will send you on a detour just to get you around the roadblocks. Look for the lessons, they are all around you.

The job gave me the flexibility to work from home. So, they set me up with a home office, and then I could come into the building whenever I wanted. Many days I would bring Xavier to work, and that old soul in a tiny body would find his way into somebody's arms on the job every time. The way they took care of me was the way I wanted to take care of other people. The work atmosphere was a treasure, but the commute was long. We sometimes would be stuck in traffic for two hours in the morning and again in the evening. Good baby or not, that commute took a toll on both of us. I hate traffic, loathe it even. Furthermore, after the terrorist attack, going to a large corporate building like that didn't sit well in my spirit, especially with my little boy in tow. I began to work from home more and eventually made the decision to resign.

I didn't stay home for long, though, with money always being a motivating factor. My aunt June Marie, my father's sister, came to Atlanta to help me care for our children, and my sister, Michelle, lived up the street. I took a job as a manager at the Eckerd Pharmacy near our house in the photo developing lab. I used my knowledge in film developing to bring up sales at that store and entice photographers and enthusiasts to use my lab.

Just by knowing the chemical makeup of the solution and properly caring for the equipment, I learned to make people's mediocre pictures look professional. I began to blow up their photos and crop them, even frame them, so they could see what they had created and boost ancillary sales. It was a small way to open the techniques of photography to my customers and increase revenue at the store. I was vying to be recognized as the best lab. But that wasn't going to come easy or quickly, so I decided to try having my own business again. My husband hated when I worked outside of our home or separate from him, but working with him didn't give me cash that I could control to pay our bills. It just gave him control of me.

My photography skills picked up a lot, and I started getting quite a few freelance gigs, mostly weddings. Professional photography was one of my dreams. I did well as a freelance photographer but eventually, I had to make the difficult decision to return home—to walk away from not just this job, but also from the insane saga that was becoming my life.

For the next five years, I stayed home with my children, busying myself with raising them and being their mom.

"God, Is This Way Too Worse?"

~uum~

Making the decision to stay at home full time was a no-brainer, but we still had realities to contend with, like paying bills and supporting our children. Our finances were still tight, and we were trying to make a volatile marriage work.

I struggled in my marriage...a lot...but I believed that I had gotten married for better or for worse. So, when things got really hard, I thought, "Who was I to say, 'No, God, this is too worse'?" Or, "This isn't the level of 'worse' that I signed up for." Truthfully, I felt my disastrous marriage was what I deserved for not listening when the Holy Spirit told me not to marry the man in the first place.

Through all of it, though, I wanted our marriage to work. I suspected that my husband was cheating, but with no solid evidence, I chose to ignore the hearsay. People had been making accusations since year one. I wouldn't believe them because I chose to believe him. Over the years, more stories—same storyline. Each time, and with each new city, all the names involved were different except one that always surfaced. His!

But when the hearsay knocks on your front door and speaks straight out of the source's mouth, you can't help but listen.

Ours was a household for entertaining. People loved to gather there to watch the big screen we enjoyed in our family movie room. My husband, being the jack of all trades, could make treasures for us out of someone else's trash. That's what he did when he created our theater room in the basement of our split-level home. Our family would often gather to watch the big screen and my cousin, Chantay, who had just moved to town from Denver, was coming over for wings and movies while her best friend was in town. My husband did most of the cooking in our household, and when we had company, his cooking was the star of the show. Literally intoxicated by what she had just been served, Chantay's friend asked for seconds and then went upstairs to load up on another helping of wings. Shortly after her, my husband went upstairs, I thought maybe to help her get something or possibly even refill his own plate. I didn't think anything of it. I may have always been oblivious, or just naïve and too trusting. I knew that I was being faithful to my husband, and I was secure in who I was as his wife. When they returned, that's all it was, and we finished the movie just as we had started, like nothing ever happened.

The next morning, a call from Chantay changed all of that.

"You're going to tell her what you told me," Chantay insisted, assuring her friend that it was the right thing to do.

On the phone, the two women described to me what made my heart sink. Just above my head, in my own kitchen, where I was watching movies with our family, he had attempted to lure her into our bedroom for a quickie. A quickie! Who in actual hell did he think he was?

"I'll be quick. I just have to see your body," were some of the words, followed by graphic details that Chantay's friend reluctantly offered me the details of my husband's inappropriate proposition.

I was enraged. It wasn't the first time, and it wasn't the second. It wasn't even the third time. What I was feeling inside was all too familiar to me. It had happened with my friend Tony, too. She and I were just getting to know each other when she told me, "Your husband says inappropriate things to me—and it makes me feel very uncomfortable—like how he wants to do certain things to me."

I knew what she was saying was true, but I cut off the friendship with her. I knew our budding friendship had to be over because I was too embarrassed to face what he had done. Ending the friendship was easier than ending my marriage.

Over the course of our marriage, he would drive many friends from me because inevitably he would speak to them inappropriately—all of them. No one was off limits, not even my best friends. The best ones stayed by me, though.

"Here we go again," I spoke calmly at first and then grew louder. Eventually, I came unglued. I pulled and tugged at my own hair and clothes. I was trying to make sense of the foolishness I was up against—once again. I walked down the hall to our room and from the basket of freshly washed clothes, I began collecting pieces and screaming. With every shirt, sock, and pant leg I let out one word per piece, stringing them together "You. Think. You. Can. Just. Do. Whatever. You. Want. To. Me? You. CAAAAANNNN'T!" I let out a shriek that made my throat instantly sore.

Then I turned my rage on him. "Every city we live in," I screamed, "you're the common denominator—from New Orleans to Houston to Atlanta. All these people are saying the same things, and they can't all be lying! You are getting out of my house!" I sent his clothes hurling down the steps like a ball of fire. At first, he started out begging me to believe him, telling me that they were liars.

I'd been through this too many times. My rage was deep and authentic. As we argued, I kept yanking clothes and throwing them down the steps. Out the front door would be their next destination. My husband was very much a person who wanted to keep his transgressions behind closed doors. Knowing his clothes were headed out the door was too much for him to process. People would know that we weren't the textbook perfect couple.

"I'm not going anywhere!" he shouted, throwing his own rage and fear of embarrassment right back at me. He then pushed me with so much force that I slid down the hallway. The only thing that stopped me was the linen closet door between the children's bedrooms and ours. He ran into our room and grabbed something he had under the bed. By now back on my feet, I begged and slithered right back to the floor. The wooden-handled axe raised into the air, and I screamed for my life. Part of me thought he wouldn't do it. Part of me believed I didn't know the face of this deranged man hovering over me. Turns out, I didn't know the depth of rage boiling inside the man standing over me. With a deep inhale of his breath, he raised the axe several inches farther into the air and lowered it with as much force as he could muster. He missed! That axe head wedged deeply into the wood floor, right between my shoulder and my ear.

Xavier, who was just two years old at the time, stood behind the door with his pacifier in his mouth, begging, "Mommy, don't cry. Mommy, you're okay. Daddy, leave Mommy alone. Mommy, don't cry." He never cried. He never screamed. He just stood there with his pacifier in his mouth trying to guide us adults in how to play nice. He's always been a protector of his mother, and he's always possessed a level of calm about him. He has always been wise beyond his years, a savior for me in many ways. I can't imagine my life without him. Today he's a sergeant in the Army, but even as a toddler, it seemed he was in training for the National Guard.

That baby I initially didn't want to give birth to was special, and it seemed everyone who came around him sensed it immediately. Whenever Xavier and I ventured to the store, perfect strangers would peer into my basket to drink from the wisdom that oozed from this baby. People I'd never laid eyes on before would walk up and tell me "I just love him." Even though I didn't know them, I knew what they meant because I felt that, too. It was as if he had been in the world before, a calm little old man set in his ways and content to just be, if you let him. He was such a perfect baby; all of my children were. He never cried too much and didn't want to be cuddled a whole lot, except by me. I would have to sit up all night to hold him in an upright position so that he would fall asleep. Some nights I would be so tired I feared I might crash to the floor and drop all ten pounds of his newborn little body. He was in training for guard duty even then, but it would be two years before we saw that manifest for the first time.

Our daughter, Brittany, who was five and a half years older than Xavier, cried hysterically as she watched the scene, helpless and afraid, not knowing what to do.

My husband wrestled to pull that axe out of the floor, and here is where I believe God was a redeemer of time.

The Bible says that God redeems time that the locusts have stolen. And while I never want to take liberties with what the Bible means, I believe God froze time in three ways for me that day in order that my life would be spared and that his could be redeemed. When I wriggled away from him, under the arm that had just tried to kill me in front of my own children, time stood still. I can't say how I got away in the time frame as he wrestled to free that axe from the wooden floor, but I know God gave me a head start. Had I moved one inch in the wrong, or right, direction, depending on how you perceive it, I would have been dead.

I ran toward our bedroom, and I remember my world froze again for a moment. In my head I knew I had gone the wrong way and was trapped in our room with no escape. I remember looking around the room for a chess move I could make. I headed for the phone. Sticking my hand out for the receiver, I knew I should call 911, but that's not what I did. I reasoned with myself. I wanted to call the police, but at the same time, I was afraid to call the police. I really didn't want the police in our business, and I knew that once I called, I wouldn't be able to take it back. I didn't want authorities to take my children and

145

put them in foster care because of the mess that they had witnessed. I didn't know what to do. There I was, contemplating, with what I feared might be a potential murderer on my tail.

Just as quickly as I thought that through, I picked up the telephone and dialed his mother's number. "Please answer," I begged, telepathically, feeling his wind at my back. I mashed the speaker button on the fax machine phone that sat next to our bed. "Mother François," I yelled, "he's trying to kill me!"

She heard the desperation in my voice. It was the only time she ever came to my rescue.

The room was loud, the air consumed with crying and pleading. I had gathered myself and plotted my next move. Hazel François, his mother, cursed and screamed at him, "Have you lost your mind? Leave that child alone!" she demanded.

"Mom, it's fine," he calmly assured her. "I'm not going to kill her. Ain't nothing going on."

Recipe Side Note...

I wonder if those days when the hours seem to drag on or when they fly by exceptionally fast, if those are days that God is redeeming time for some other soul like mine. Next time I sense that time has hit a slow pace, I think I'll whisper a prayer for someone in need.

It was a crazy scene. He literally had been acting like a madman, but once he heard his mother's voice, he snapped out of it. "I'm not going to hurt her," he spoke calmly to her. "We are going to call you back."

As soon as he hung up the phone the madman was back.

In what felt like something out of a horror movie, our daughter, Lauren, jumped between us. She was willing to intervene, even though she was only twelve at the time. Then our other daughter got behind her and stood in the middle of the hallway to slow their father down. "Run, Mom!"

Time lapse: sixty seconds at best.

I sprinted down the hallway, trying to stay on my feet. I don't even remember whether I had shoes on. We lived in a split-level house with a set of stairs and then a landing, followed by another set of stairs. I jumped the first set of stairs in one leap. All I knew was that I needed to get outside if I wanted to live. He wouldn't do anything to me if others might be watching. Once I was safely outside, Brittany raced past me and across the street to bang on a neighbor's door for help. Our neighbors had heard the commotion, so they opened the door and whisked me inside.

The Ethiopian family who lived across the street came to my rescue. Their culture was so different, she was confused by what was going on between my husband and me, but at the same time, she understood what she had to do. Her sympathy was extended at a level I had never experienced from her before. She called her husband, and he came home. They kept me at their house until my husband calmed down. When François' sister heard what had happened, she told him to come to her house. He complied. When I left my kind neighbors' house, I was still afraid to go home, but my sister-in-law assured me that my husband would stay with her for the night. I slept in our bed, eyes wide open and terrified all that night.

That incident was not the first time that things had gotten physical between us. The first year we were married, I got so angry with him that I punched his chest. He grabbed my hands, and said, "Stop hitting me, or I'm going to hit you back!"

I never hit him again. I believed what he said; he would hit me back. But I wanted to pack up our kids and leave—the one I gave birth to and the kids that came with the marriage. I couldn't see leaving them behind because they trusted me. At that point, they were as much mine as they were his.

When things got quiet, my husband returned home, but he did not come alone. His sister and her husband had come along to make sure things were really calm. There in the presence of his sister and brother-in-law, I received a tearful apology. Hesitant to feel safe so quickly, I proceeded with caution. He seemed sorry that he had caused a raucous within our home that had invited his family's involvement. I was beaten up on the inside that I had signed up for better or worse, so who was I to be asking, "God, this is way too worse?"

I was guided by a determination to be successful at marriage. Success, by my definition, would have simply meant 'til death do us part. I never reconciled that death should not come at the hands of the one who was supposed to love, honor, and keep himself only unto me. Those were part of our vows, but all I was focused on in the moment was staying in it through the good *and* the bad. All I could focus on was that love bears all things and that love never fails (1 Corinthians 13:7–8).

What I hadn't been able to see by then was that love is also patient, love is kind, and that love is not easily provoked (1 Corinthians 13:4–5). That day before had been so loud, but the following day things were a lot calmer. I remember retreating to our bedroom and talking through the things that happened. From that conversation, we decided that it was safe for my in-laws to return to their lives, and we would have a heartfelt talk before returning to our regularly scheduled programming.

In the aftermath of what had just happened, I turned for advice to the one woman I knew could understand. My parents had related experiences before my father turned back to God. Sitting on the porch, I was trying to reconcile how I would stay with a man that had just tried to kill me and made the call.

"Hi, Mom!" I sang, a little nervous about the call.

"Hey, Mignon," she sang back.

I don't know why I thought I would find compassion when I told my mother all that had just occurred. But I'm a mother too, and I know it is never okay to watch your daughter suffer, especially when you know her suffering firsthand. I thought she would be empathetic because she had experienced things like this before—things about which she had never divulged the details. That is, until this moment. My mother had never told us what had happened between her and my father, only that she had left him. Flashbacks as I told her my story moved her to confess the truth about the horrific things that, to this day, are not mine to repeat.

"I cannot sit here and tell you that it's fine," she spoke with matter-of-fact fury in her throat. She begged me to leave him. She so desperately wanted me out of that marriage, not wanting her daughter to live in trauma. Better yet, she just wanted her daughter to be living, unmarred.

We were renting the house we lived in, a surprise gift my mother had financed about a year after we moved to Lawrenceville. Her plan was to sell it to us after we got on our feet, for the same price she had paid. The house was a HUD foreclosure she was thinking about buying when she called us over with the kids to have a look around. "What do you think?" she asked.

"Oh, we like it," we told her, excited for what she was going to do with her newly uncovered gem. I immediately started dreaming out loud about what she could do with the place when she stuck out a set of keys and said, "It's yours. Just pay the note on it every month."

After the axe episode, she wanted us out of her house. If my husband was going to mistreat her daughter—she wasn't going to provide a place for it to happen.

Seeing that I was resigned to stay with him, she told me, "Well, if you stay, I'm not staying with you." She wanted her house back. Since my mother meant what she said, we realized that besides needing a new start, we also were going to need a new place to live. She gave us some time to figure things out. We made the decision to leave Atlanta and sold his tools to get money to move. Eventually, my mom put the house up for sale, and we made a move to Nashville hoping to start a new life.

Until writing this book, this was a part of my story I had never revealed publicly. Most people only know that my family came to Nashville in search of a better life. A precious few people knew we had experienced some times of turmoil in our relationship, but nobody, except those children, knew what I really went through on the journey to becoming me. I think a lot of times people want your life, and they envy what you've been able to accomplish. What they don't know, and don't want to endure, is what it takes to get to what they see.

I was fighting for my life in those days—sometimes literally.

Despite the fact that my husband wasn't a good money manager, he was the bread winner, and as such he wanted control over our money. He wanted me to stay at home, too. Trying to please my husband, I bore all these things in relative silence.

It's hard sometimes to relive these painful memories and to think of myself as having been so foolish. I allowed the man I'd married to run roughshod over our finances and our lives. But I was young and determined to win at marriage and at money. That was a long-fought battle more than twenty-one years in the making. It took me that long to recognize that we were never going to win at both of those things, at least not at the same time and not as a couple.

Our decision to move to Nashville was also a decision to step away from being self-employed. It was to be a new start for our marriage and for our finances. So, before we left Atlanta, I'd made a conscious decision and a choice for myself when I told him, "If anything like this happens in Nashville, don't ever talk to me again."

In Nashville, though, it just got worse.

Gentle Reminder to Self...

"If you don't like your life, change it!
Stop living in limbo."

Bishop T.D. Jakes

Same Scenario, Different Day, City

They say that insanity is doing the same thing and expecting different results. My income wasn't enough to adequately sustain our family and we were living insanely—mainly because nothing had changed in the dynamic of our household. We didn't change anything about our relationship, but we decided to change our location.

We decided to leave Atlanta, not recognizing that as long as the household dynamic didn't change, nothing else would change. If you're using the same recipe for chocolate cake, it really doesn't matter where you bake it—New Orleans, Houston, Atlanta, or Nashville—you end up with the same chocolate cake.

We looked at several places on the map, and we settled on Nashville as our new home. I had a best friend there, and it was close enough to New Orleans and Atlanta that I could be near my family while offering some distance to give our family space to reset and recoup without the influence of anyone else's opinion.

When we moved to Nashville, a cabinet-making company had promised my husband an executive level position; however, as soon as we arrived, the job fell through. The division he was to head never materialized. The company offered him a job as an installer, a position he had experience with, but he soon quit. We had sold all his tools to get enough money to move to Nashville and the promise of a better life minus the physical labor. It seemed ideal, except for the fact that my husband really wasn't equipped to take on the task he was facing.

There we were, yet again, about to descend into what we had been trying to escape by leaving New Orleans, Houston, and Atlanta. It felt like Struggle was a squatter who had invaded our lives and refused to go away. It was time for a come-to-Jesus moment with a Higher Authority. "God, you're going to have to show me. You're going to have to provide the answer to me because my husband is not going to participate in really trying to make things better. He's not going to help me. Just give me whatever is left, and I'll try to figure out something to do with that."

My husband had never been particularly good with money, spending on luxuries while our needs went unmet. Still, he was hell-bent on not being embarrassed as the provider for our family. He didn't ever want me to tell anybody the truth about what was going on in our lives. We were often living without electricity, we often didn't have water, and many times we didn't know where our next meal was coming from. And though we always ate, sometimes that wouldn't be until well after our children should have been sleeping. My husband spent a lot of time going to pawn shops, pawning things that he would never get back. I remember the day he went to pawn his dad's watch. His father was one of the first Black conductors on the Southern Pacific Railroad, as I have been told, and he had kept time by that very pocket watch, which was given to my husband on the day he buried his father. He cried when he had to pawn that watch. But as hard as that decision was, nothing ever changed with regard to his spending.

I had compassion for what my husband felt in that moment. I know that was a hard thing to do, but I really wanted to tell him, "You give up your very legacy for things that don't matter, because in the end you'll say, 'Oh, I'm doing it, so my kids get to eat.' No!

You were supposed to make sure your kids ate before you bought stuff you didn't need. You don't take care of us first." I didn't say anything, though, because no one wants to be kicked when they're already down. But I was so tired of our family living on Down Street.

We often did not have enough for rent, or to buy groceries, but somehow, we did manage to have enough money for my husband to purchase expensive new speakers, which he apparently thought we needed more than food or shelter. We also managed to have money enough for him to buy me flowers. Make no mistake, I love fresh-cut flowers. It's a luxury he taught me to appreciate. But I never wanted flowers more than field trip money for my children or electricity to turn on light switches or water running in our faucets for hot baths. I spit a lot of rage at him in those days and, looking back, I can admit that I contributed just as much to the demise of a man who ultimately wanted me and my demands out of his life.

"If you buy me flowers one more time," I threatened, "I'm going to throw them away. Stop buying me flowers! You take care

Recipe Side Note...

"You may be able to catch bees with honey, but you can sure attract and keep them with bright flowers."

Maybe the flowers could have been a key to helping our relationship sustain if I had chosen to see them differently. Maybe it was up to me all along to produce the honey. In fact, I called him Honey more than his given name.

of yourself first and what you want and then buy me flowers that I don't need. I want more for these kids. They don't deserve this!"

Desperate for food in our pantry and to make ends meet however we could, my husband suggested that I apply for food stamps, so I complied. We were denied. We needed emergency money, and we were denied. Just thinking about it can still bring tears to my eyes. I told my husband, "If you ever decide we need to apply for Food Stamps again, go apply yourself." The application process made me feel like I had been stripped naked and then told I wasn't good enough.

The experience made me feel like I had lifted the veil on our lives to tell a welfare worker that, in fact, we didn't have any money in our bank account, our mortgage was behind, our lights were cut off, and I didn't have money to put gas in my car to get my children to school. Still, we didn't qualify. Feeling stripped of all dignity, I walked out the doors of the food stamp office, wearing my shame as if I was walking naked in front of a room full of strangers.

I didn't know how we would ever escape swimming in the mire of never having enough, or even having what we needed. I was scrappy, and I was hungry. At the same time, I didn't want to be a victim, and I didn't want to blame my husband for what I was participating in. My parents had always stood by to be my helper when needed, to be a savior, if I needed it. But at this point, even my parents were done with our chaotic financial condition.

So much money had been misappropriated that my parents had loaned us money to sustain our family. He would tell them things like, "I have this big contract, and they aren't paying me on it yet. I need you to loan me some money to get it finished." And like a red bull with wings, that money would fly away, never to be repaid.

Finally, my parents decided they'd had enough. They were done saving me from something they felt I kept choosing to stay in. They recognized that if they continued to bail us out, they would be bankrolling our dysfunction—not to mention that they never got back any of the money they were promised. My mom called that "fattening frogs for snakes."

Through all the financial ups and downs, though, I always believed that my husband would eventually get it right. I always believed he would finally listen to wisdom—a.k.a. me. It never happened. Time for another "come to Jesus" with the Lord. "I'm not staying in this apartment for more than a year. I will do whatever I have to do, but if You want me to stay in this marriage with this man, You are going to have to make a way. You said that You didn't want me to be enslaved. I am living as a slave—to whenever the electric company decides to turn my lights off, to whenever the landlord decides to put an eviction notice on our door, and to whenever the loan company decides to repossess our cars."

I have had so many cars repossessed. I don't think anyone should ever have to experience the feeling of dreaded surprise that comes from having the car you've been paying for taken away.

I laid it out before God. It was time for my own come-to-Jesus moment with myself: "I'm done participating in this life." I believe that declaration was the catalyst for my progression into a new life where financial struggle no longer took up residence under my roof. It also fueled the demise of our marriage.

I didn't know how to tell my husband what I desperately needed, mainly because I felt like he didn't care anyway. At that point, my focus had become taking care of our kids.

I had hit survival mode. I began hiding money and doing whatever I could to survive.

"The Ugliest Little House in Nashville"

"It is only with the heart that one can see clearly...."
~ *Hans Christian Andersen,* The Ugly Duckling

We were living in an apartment that wasn't nearly big enough for our family of eight, but we were getting by until we could do better. One day while working, my husband spotted an intriguing house in a section of North Nashville, very close to downtown. The houses there boasted an architectural style that reminded us of New Orleans. The sidewalks were brick, and the homes were full of character. We desperately wanted to buy in the historic Germantown neighborhood, even though he had been warned to leave by dusk or, if he stayed, watch his back at night. That didn't deter us either. In fact, we didn't believe in the fear factor. We had come here with a plan to move our children to the inner city for the richness in culture we wanted them to know.

My husband invited me to meet him for lunch at a little local restaurant on the corner of Sixth and Monroe Streets in Germantown. He had eaten there before and thought the food to be impressive and the wait staff incredible. When he picked me up, I could tell he was really excited. The reality of what we had given up by coming here had not yet fully materialized. We remained optimistic that Nashville was going to offer opportunities that the other places simply hadn't or couldn't, I'm not sure which. Probably they hadn't because we never stuck to anything long enough for game changers to know what we had to offer. Or maybe we couldn't because we never stuck to anything long enough for the opportunities to arise.

Several months into our move, my husband was holding a regular employed job installing cabinets all over the Salemtown and Germantown neighborhoods, two adjacent communities enjoying booming growth and transformation. I use the word "enjoying" sort of frivolously here as the only ones likely enjoying the transformation were the property owners. Most of these North Nashville residents didn't have the luxury of owning their properties, mostly due to redlining. The uptick in construction mostly meant the longtime residents were finding themselves misplaced and displaced in a situation they were powerless to change or circumvent.

Traveling over the Jefferson Street Bridge, I could sense the downtown Nashville skyline change on the horizon. As he drove us to the restaurant for lunch, I felt as if we had crossed over into a jewel that I had not been privy to discovering on my previous exploratory travels. Whenever we would move into new areas, I would hop in my car and get lost, literally. I carried a large industrial map with me and would MapQuest the area. I would print destinations the best I could before leaving home but would always venture to lose myself on the streets of a new town. To me, it's the best way to get to know a new place and all it has to offer.

The place where we were about to have lunch, though, hadn't been on my radar. How had I missed it? We turned through the neighborhood and "Oohh'd" and "Ahhh'd" at the architecture. Woven into the quaint community were some historical landmarks, tiny ornate edifices, and churches that reminded me of home. We meandered through the few blocks that made up the two historic neighborhoods, both of which were obviously in the throes of overhaul. There were carpenters' trailers, flooring vans, and roofers' trucks on every block. There were tractors and backhoes and arborists and landscapers. Also sharing space in this hub of activity were industrial plants and meat butchering. What had taken him so long to bring me here?

Getting lost in time and more excited with each turn, I nudged. "Where's the house you want me to see?" Soon it would be time to pick up Xavier from the Mother's Day Out program I had found at a megachurch in Brentwood, the suburban area where I had been exploring as a suitable place for our family to move. Left on Madison, down two blocks, right turn on Sixth Avenue North—that's when he began to slow the car to a halt.

"There, on the left!" he pointed.

"That?" I grimaced.

Had he guided me on a tour through all this grandeur just to lead me to the ugliest little house in Nashville? It was painted at least three different shades of tan-brown and had a green dormer peeking out from the roof. The fence was trimmed in barbed wire and the trees were so overgrown you couldn't even see how big or small the house actually was.

Recipe Note to My Married Self...

You could have kept that last comment to yourself. This is what you call tearing your husband down to shreds sliver by sliver, but you won't know that you participated in the decline of your marriage until it had been over for many years.

"You brought me out here to see this?" I was neither excited nor amused. "That restaurant you promised had better be better than this!"

We rolled down to the end of the block and he parked the car. The restaurant front-of-house maître d' was a woman who introduced herself as Brenda. A tall black woman with braces and dark hair, she was warm and welcoming. She was happy to see us, I could tell, but she maintained a level of professional reserve. She wore laughter and joy like a hat on her head. As the popular little lunch spot filled up, it became obvious that all the regular patrons knew her, and she knew them. This little eatery became the neighborhood gathering place for the duration of the lunch hour. Service was quick, and the food was delicious and affordable.

My husband had a knack for finding a great meal on a budget midday. He believed wholeheartedly that eating well for lunch for the price of eating at a fast-food chain was one of the luxuries he would not be denied for all his hard work.

Sitting by the window, I admired the detail of the small cottages that lined that end of the block. They reminded me of what I had always wanted in New Orleans—a home Uptown where I could walk to the local bistro, tie my dog to a leash, stroll inside for lunch, and then stroll back into our home to carry on with managing our household until the children filed back in from school. That's what these people had and that's what I wanted, too. It was home in the heart of Nashville.

As I was quickly falling in love with the neighborhood, I thought about the little ugly house my husband showed me, with its awkward roofline that was dwarfed in the shadow of the eight- or twelve-unit apartment building next door. Had I judged this place prematurely, I considered thoughtfully. "Take me back to that house," I said.

Moments later we were making our way back down to the house, meeting the real estate agent for a tour inside. They showed us what they projected would be an ideal property for a complete renovation or a demolition project to place a restaurant.

A restaurant?

The inside was in worse shape than the outside. It reeked! It was dark and dank and smelled old and mildewy. As I stepped through the halls I tripped in a hole and dropped a few inches into the floor. As he helped me out of the hole, I whispered in my husband's ear, "I love it!"

When I wrote the proposal to buy the house, I told my husband, "If the house is for us, it's ours no matter what. Let me write a deal, and if they accept it, they accept it. If they don't, it's not ours. What do we have to lose?"

My deal included being honest with the sellers: "I need you to owner finance." Then I said something to the effect of, "I don't want to pay a note for a year, because I'm going to need that money to fix up this house."

I was encouraged to make such a bold proposal because I believed that half of my ideal offer was displayed on the for-sale sign

Recipe Note to My Naïve Self...

"People don't owe you anything, Mignon. They don't owe you care about your situation or your needs. They owe them. And as you begin to realize that you owe yourself that same level of commitment, you'll stop expecting your own lack of preparation to be a cause of aggravation to someone other than yourself. Soon enough, you'll hang a sign that reads, "Your urgency is not my emergency," from the window of your soul.

anyway: "Owner Financing Available." I was so green. Available, guaranteed, and approved are all separate concepts that I read into that sign as meaning accessible for me.

The house had been condemned, and it rained more on the inside than it did on the outside. There were several communal toilets in what seemed to be a dormitory-style bathroom, similar to that of a military latrine, toward the back of the house. Of course, that would have to go, I noted as I made plans in my mind for our new home. Each room had a door with a lock and key. Walls overrun with old newspapers stuffed within its crevices. The ceilings were tall, and each room boasted an inoperable fireplace that I hoped could be restored (but no such luck). The floors were weak and gave under pressure. As we explored the house and fell in love with every square foot, it became something worth going after.

"Do you understand there's going to be restaurants here? People want to get this property so they can turn it into a restaurant." The owners who scoffed at our offer thought we were crazy to make such an audacious proposal.

We didn't know anything about the possibility of restaurants vying for this property or that the offer we were proposing constituted our being crazy. We were making our best offer, and that was around $60,000 or $80,000.

The asking price was $140,000, but I thought that was highway robbery. Germantown had been a predominantly Black area of town for many years. Because of redlining, many families of color were blocked from purchasing homes, as loans were not being offered to purchase or remodel these neighborhoods with properties mostly held by slum lords. This was where we were determined to make our home, even though we couldn't afford to buy a house here or in any other area. Since we couldn't qualify for a mortgage loan, this property with its owner-financing potential posed a unique opportunity that I wasn't willing to let slip away easily.

Truthfully, we were lucky these people were even talking to us about buying a home. Looking at our financial standing on paper, we honestly were wasting their time and ours. Still, something in me believed that if we could get the owners to finance, like the real estate sign touted, and for a price more in the range of $80,000, we might find a forever home for our children in this new little big town.

We thought we were making a fair deal and the seller thought we were losing our minds. Better yet he thought I was a real estate tycoon who drove a hard bargain, especially with what came out of my mouth next. "No one is going to turn this into a restaurant," I told one of the sellers. "Nobody really cares about this. I want it for my family because this area reminds me of New Orleans."

Funny what people think of you when you walk by faith. Blinded by my own insecurities and naïve to what God was getting ready to do, I had no idea what a great door He was opening in my favor.

The owners promptly turned down my offer, but their initial rebuff was not enough to deter me. I took some dirt from the ground, put it a plastic bag, and began to pray over the property that I was claiming in faith for my family. Some weeks went by and the house kind of left the forefront of my attention. I was used to not being taken seriously. Besides, I figured that God had a bigger plan than the one we had devised for that house.

A call from the real estate agent for the property reinvigorated my faith. He asked if we were still interested. The last time we had driven past the house I'd thought, "Oh my gosh, that house hasn't sold. Maybe I need to give back this dirt. If it's not my house, maybe I'm holding up somebody from getting their blessing."

I spiritually released the property. I was no stranger to disappointment, so I had determined to let the house go because it must not have been ours. And if it was ours, nothing could stop us from acquiring it.

When the real estate agent asked if we were still interested, my husband and I looked at each other and, with a definite hint of sarcasm, asked, "You mean the house that people were breaking down the doors to get to? The one that's going to have restaurants there? That property?"

He said, not engaging in our cynicism, "Yes, the owner wants to talk to you."

We met with Tim, the seller, at his facility, and he offered our family a deal. "If you do the renovations on another property of mine, I will give you the $10,000 you need down for your house." Because we had asked for no money down, Tim offered, "I'll give you the money that you need to pay down, and I'll finance it for you."

We took the deal.

"Let me make this clear," Tim added conditionally. "You're not going to get any money. All you're going to get is credit for the work that you're going to do on this other property. In exchange, I'm going to give you the $10,000 that you need. I'll finance this one for you."

Tim took us to the property that he wanted us to work on and told us what needed to be done.

My husband was an expert at renovations. He truly was a jack of all trades. You know how they say, "Jack of all trades, but master of none?" He really was a master of all. He could do anything. He got to work on the property and along the way started offering Tim more thoughts on what needed to happen. Our entire family showed up to do the work. Since it was the middle of the summer, the children were out of school. Even three-year-old Xavier had his little tool belt on. I still have a picture of him from that very day looking adorable, wearing his tiny tool belt. He was serious about his work, too. To this day, he's still good with his hands, and at age twenty-one, he began an engineering career in the Army. When Xavier is home, he also serves as a helping hand around the city and at the bakery, managing production. In fact, all our children learned how to work with their hands as we did renovation work. From laying tile, cutting millwork, and fishing wire through walls to run electrical wire and speaker cable, my girls and boys became skillful at home renovations.

At the outset of the renovations, I cautioned my children that I would "choke them out" or "kill 'em dead" if their grandparents heard a peep about our new place. The way we had moved to Nashville on the heels of the turmoil that we left behind, my mother would have been on the first thing smoking to collect me had she seen what we had purchased as our dream home.

But our renovation plan did include inviting my father to come and stay with us for a while to help complete our house project in Germantown once the renovation was further along. Hurricane Katrina hit New Orleans in 2005, around the time we were getting into the full swing of rehabbing our 1800-square feet of ownership. In this regard, and for others, I've always seen Katrina as the "perfect" storm and felt blessed that she blew my dad right into my lap.

Before the hurricane hit, he had been too busy to commit the time to come help. He had been working as a general contractor in New Orleans since he retired from AT&T, and he was always busy with projects. My dad was a generous helper and that kept him slammed, booked, and busy. If an elderly person couldn't afford what he was charging, he would ask, "How much you got?" Whatever they could afford would be the price he charged.

He often put young boys to work to teach them a skill and simultaneously help in the community. If he felt your design needed his version of an upgrade, you got it—at his own expense. With his services in great demand there, we were hardly ever going to get that man loosed from his schedule. But I prayed for help, and my answer came in a terrible storm that would displace him, and the entire city of New Orleans, for several weeks. Some residents were displaced for months, others for years, and in some parts of my hometown, "normal" has not returned even eighteen years later. For that he, as well as the rest of us, would never be the same.

My dad came to Nashville and worked on our home for several weeks. By the time Daddy had arrived, we had cleaned up the place a lot and had a solid plan in place, complete with blueprints and permits.

Not that we had to be so far along for him to appreciate what we had going on. It's just that he would have called my mother and her vision wasn't as blurred as his when it came to seeing things my way.

Finally, things were looking up and I was comfortable letting both my parents in on what we had been up to. Before the hurricane, we'd kept my dad in the dark for a variety of reasons. Sometimes dads have to be informed on a need-to-know basis when it comes to their daughters. At least that was my experience.

Now that the storm had displaced him, he needed something fulfilling to do, and truth be told, I felt he owed me that—to come and just be my daddy.

We were also still working Tim's other property as if we were going to live there ourselves. Tim was either so inspired or guilt-ridden at the sight of our entire family showing up to do the work that he offered us cash to keep us afloat while we worked to earn our down payment and financing for the house.

"How are y'all coming along here?" He was genuinely concerned about our family. "You're working on my property. You know I'm not giving you any money, right? You're not showing up to any other job. How are you living?"

The truth was that we were living on faith, going to pawn shops, and surviving off red beans and sandwiches for meals. God provided manna for us in ways I can't even begin to go back and recall. Thinking back on it, I don't even know how we made it. You can't see the picture for the frame, right? That was our life. We were just in it.

As we worked to get the down payment, Tim would always seem to slide in and bless our family with something financial, even though every week he would remind us, "I'm not giving you anything." Yet, he did.

I had heard a similar story taught in a lesson my mom often referenced in worship or with her Sabbath school class to instill the value of integrity. The story was about two people who were each sent to build a house. One completed the job by cutting corners, but the other built the house as if it was their own. When the two workers finished, they were given the keys to the very houses that they had built. The one who had put in blood, sweat, and tears, believing it was the right thing to do, was rewarded with a beautiful new home that was well built. The other worker ended up getting a house that was shoddy because they did poor work. I think that's what happened to our family. We were showing up every day, faithfully and meticulously doing the work. I wanted a home of our own so badly that I put my own spin on that home. I would say, "Ooh! This would be cool if the floors looked like this."

My husband trusted me to pick the flooring. Together, we had great ideas. I could have ideas, and he would say, "This is how you execute that." He would take my ideas and make them tangible.

"If this were your house, what would you do?" he would ask me.

I lived for pouring through a renovation magazine and the promise of rehab within its pages: *This Old House, House Beautiful, Southern Living*, and *Architectural Digest*. My heart gets happy just thinking about the gift of imagination within those pages. Even if it wasn't for me, a girl could still dream. I was content to dream for myself and everyone around me if allowed. Because I wasn't holding the purse strings, I let my imagination soar for those projects. Then, knowing just what it would take and how much it would cost, along with what he could save, he would execute the project as if he were doing it for me.

Working that way ended up being money in our pockets. We got the financing for the house as well as the down payment money that Tim had promised us.

We moved into our dream house, complete with a half bathroom—a tub and a toilet, no sink, no coverings on the floor, no finishes on the wall. Our "extra bathroom" was an unfinished room where we had placed an orange Home Depot bucket with a toilet seat attached. The tub doubled as our sink. The walls, absent of sheetrock and sparsely covered here and there with sporadically broken plaster or some version thereof, were either cinder block walls or exposed wood. Nowadays, people are actually paying for a similar version of what we had then, a design called shiplap, only ours wasn't backed by insulation and wasn't neat to look at. The gaps in the spacing let in cold and exposed pieces of newspaper that had been stuffed in between the spaces to keep out the elements. I thought that it was horrible, I wanted sheet rock. The flooring was exposed plywood we had laid ourselves to bring closure and comfort as we saved every extra dollar for materials in our new home. I'll never forget the day we were working in that house and little Xavier walked over to me with a present in his hand, proudly sharing his newfound glass treasure. "Here, Mommy. I found you something." It was a crack vial. Immediately examining his hands for cuts or any sign that he had been injured, I was horrified—enough to motivate me to keep working harder to improve conditions for our family.

My husband landed a job with Tim and had become one of his lead foremen or carpenters after we turned over that first project better than the price deserved and more than what the owner could have expected. After he would finish working for Tim all day, he would come home, and our family would work on our house at night. We took weekend pilgrimages to Dalton, Georgia, to buy tile for our flooring at well below retail pricing. The children worked their summer days hauling bricks that had been knocked down from an old fireplace to open the layout of what had been labeled office on the front room of the house. The layout of our new home was choppy. It had been a rooming house in its most recent past, and people could rent a room for an hour or by the day. Boy, if those walls could talk!

Each floorboard was passed through a wood shaper to restore the original floors that had surprisingly been mostly preserved under layers of carpet and plywood. After removing the nails by hand, each board was planed to reveal its original oak splendor. I had always dreamed of owning an historic Victorian home and this was going to be a close shot. The children cut individual blocks of wood meticulously at one-inch spacing to create a dentil molding reminiscent of the period. Making a condemned building our dream home was a slow, tedious process, but soon we had sheetrock and a kitchen, and the house was beginning to look like a home. It was always a work in progress as we were growing in it, but finally we had something of our own that nobody would be able to take, or so we thought. I later learned that indeed was wishful thinking.

"Go Make Cupcakes"

The long days of working outside the home during the day and renovating our home at night took a toll on our whole family. Climbing, scratch that, dragging himself onto the porch early one evening as the summer sun painted the sky gradient shades of orange, purple, and pink, my husband didn't look well. I saw something different in the man I married at age nineteen. He looked a dirty shade of gray and very pale under the five o'clock shadow that was boring through his face at just the right time of day. Something in my soul told me to pray. That's what I did, in that moment, before he even hit the front door. I began to ask God to help me help him. At first, I just thought he was working too hard. He was declining in my eyes, and I was genuinely concerned about him. I even worried that he might be dying. What I didn't realize at the time was that he was, in a matter of speaking, dying. He was dying to me. He would not be with me for much longer.

I asked God for something I could do to help my husband make ends meet, and then I remembered that guy on the radio who had people screaming with excitement about having erased their debt using his advice. I wanted what they were screaming about. That was the beginning of my independence.

The guy on the radio had a voice I could listen to and a message that was familiar: financial peace with a biblical foundation. My parents had taught me the very things he was preaching on the radio. Growing up, we listened to a lot of talk radio in the car with our mom on the twenty- to thirty-minute commute from New Orleans east to Canal Street and Broad where she worked. From there, we would catch the public service route to school. On those drives, we listened, a lot, to Paul Harvey and The Rest of the Story. When we lived in Atlanta, I lived for the money, savings, and travel deals from consumer advocate and money expert Clark Howard. Once we moved to Nashville, I was in hot pursuit of something similar that I could learn from the car as I navigated my way around the city. When I heard the clamoring, yelling, and all-out hoopla of a family that had just paid their way out of debt, I was intrigued to know more as the show was signing off for the day.

Dave Ramsey's financial advice to listeners included baby steps that people could take on the journey to financial stability. He called it freedom, something I resonated with because I knew that our family was bound by indebtedness. I paid attention as Dave advised listeners to start the path to getting their finances in order by making sure they have enough to take care of their four walls or household needs—a roof over their head, food in the pantry, transportation to get to work, and all those kinds of things. My favorite part, and the gamechanger for me, was the envelope system he suggested. Using that system, you take your money and put it in envelopes so that you can snowball paying off your debt. Once your necessities are taken care of, you then throw all of your money into paying off the smallest bill that you have first. Once the smallest bill is paid in full, you start knocking out your other debts, from the smallest to the biggest.

But that's not what I loved most about those envelopes. My family was way too far behind and way too deep in debt to be focusing on what sounded like a snowball fight with money. Dave's advice was simple, and I could start on it that day. I didn't have to pay for access; it was free. Even better, if I could find my way to a church that offered his Financial Peace University, I could take his course for free. Still, that's not even what I loved most about those envelopes. Dave's plan to pay my bills by saving the money in the envelopes and keeping my money out of the bank was sage advice I could cling to. Sure, he talked about investing and saving and retirement plans, but where we were financially at that time, those were all foreign concepts for me. I could barely keep my bank account out of overdraft, and when it did go into overdraft, a mere one-cent miscalculation could send our finances reeling into an avalanche of enormous fees owed to the bank. My money was so funny (read: unstable), it seemed that the banks waited on me like vultures, paying those debts first that would send me into the negative. Fees in excess of forty dollars for being even one cent shy. The idea of taking twenty dollars here and five dollars there meant that the money I had in hand could be used how I deemed necessary and for what I needed to get ahead. When I stopped worrying about the loudest wheel squeaking, I started paying attention to what mattered most—my children, our family, and our four walls.

I began to write down advice that Dave gave. I soaked in the advice he offered as if it was school for people who were struggling financially—just like me. I lived for the moments just before they would sign off for the chance to hear the debt-free screams. Their testimonies gave me encouragement and hope. They would tell him, "I have been doing the baby steps and I have paid off a gazillion dollars in debt in two years, eighteen months. I tried this thing or that thing, and it worked for me." So I figured if they could move beyond their financial hole, so could I. Dave would be so excited to hear about what they had accomplished. It was like having a coach get you pumped.

During those days I spent a lot of time in my car mostly shuttling my children back and forth to school. I would drive up to our house and sit in my car—sometimes for thirty minutes, sometimes for an hour, or sometimes just long enough to hear the end of the segment I was listening to. I needed to know what I was supposed to do. I felt as if my life depended on paying attention to the advice these people were receiving.

One of the things I had heard Dave Ramsey suggest on his radio show was that people can help themselves get out of debt by having a bake sale or a garage sale. We didn't have anything we could sell because we had sold everything we had to get to Nashville.

"An idea was born when I turned on the TV;
my life began when I turned the TV off."

~ Mignon François

Sitting in the makeshift kitchen-den combo of my affluent Germantown neighborhood home, before the sun ever crept over the horizon, I found myself searching. There I was, drowning in debt and brokenness, about to lose everything I had, including this house. I secretly wondered, well maybe it wasn't secretly. I am sure I complained to my mom, my sisters, and my friends, likely the neighbors, too, and sometimes whoever would listen about the sick and tired nature of my existence. So likely everyone knew I needed something to change. Everyone including God Himself.

There, alone in the dim light, comforted only by the glow of forty watts emanating from the corner lamp, I surfed the television channels for what now was more than a month of waking up at this crazy time every day. Like clockwork, or maybe like the movie *Groundhog Day*, because it seems way too silly for me to say clockwork when describing the actions of the clock doing its job, my eyes popped open at 3:17 a.m. Thinking back, sometimes I remember being jolted by an alarm that never sounded, at least not for anyone else to hear, or a nudge in a dream that manifested as me waking up on time at 3:17 to do the same thing I had done tonight and every night before it.

Back door? Locked. Check!

Stove? Off. Check!

Kids breathing? Check! Check! Check! Check! Check!

Five of the six of them were tucked securely and soundly. The sixth one we had left in Atlanta, and had I thought he'd answer his momma at 3:17 in the morning, I would have called. At eighteen and living on his own, he had probably just dragged himself indoors moments earlier, if I'm gauging him right.

Front door? Locked. Check!

Then the sleepy walk back down our fifty-foot hallway that was paved in bricks we had hand cut from Saltillo pavers we purchased in Georgia on the weekends when we had saved up enough to afford to buy a few more. Saltillo isn't expensive by most people's standards, especially those privy to home ownership and in neighborhoods like the one where we were living by then. At the time it may have cost sixty-nine cents per 12"x12" square. But saving to get that, for our family, those stones we had laid ourselves might as well have been some exotic marble or stone because of everything we had scraped, scratched, and clawed to get. What I loved most about the terracotta clay tiles was their imperfect shapes only enhanced by the occasional print of a dog's paw impression left overnight if they wandered across wet uncured clay.

Normally, I would head back off to bed after making my rounds to stare at the ceiling, sometimes for hours, before falling back to sleep. This particular time, I found myself wide awake and ready for whatever moments I could steal alone in front of the TV. Cable wasn't a luxury we were blessed to have, so television at this hour mostly meant paid programming or PBS. I love television. Correction, I loved television. (In my head I said that like Rafiki in the *Lion King* when young Simba asks if the wise old sage had known his father.) I wasn't a mother who limited my children's time in front of the television, or made them turn it off while doing their homework. I learned from the television and often used it to keep me company when no one else was around.

Unable to locate the remote, I glided my fingers beneath the edge of the thirty-two-inch television to change channels and found that PBS was in the middle of a fundraising campaign. Besides February's Black History Month, fundraising on PBS offers the best programming in my opinion, and I suspected this night would be no different.

"The morning breeze has something to tell you. Do not go back to sleep." The tall, thin, older white gentleman paced the stage in what looked to be a sermon series or a seminar, not quite sure which. Dressed in a black sweater he addressed a full auditorium of eager listeners who took notes as he spoke.

Unsure I wanted to hear what the morning breeze had to say, I again looked casually for the remote and passively listened at the same time.

"The morning breeze has something to tell you. Do not go back to sleep," he repeated for the second time.

Now I was desperately searching for that remote. I had been raised in a strict religious and devout Christian home and I didn't know anything about a morning breeze, neither was I interested in what it had to say. My desperate search never lured me far off that coach or back onto my feet before the man spoke up again.

"God is trying to speak to you, and this is the only time you'll be silent enough to hear him," the man said. And with that he grabbed my full attention.

I had been asking God to visit me, to give me a sign and a plan to help us out of the mess we were in. A flip back through my spiral-bound journal reminded me of how loud our lives were back then. All the yelling and commotion wasn't just coming from the kids. My husband and I were pumping up the volume a lot...every day.

Stunned a little that I was listening to a man talk directly to me from the television about hearing God, had me superglued to the edge of my seat. My legs shook as I prayed for a station break for fundraising. I had to pee really bad, but I didn't want to miss a thing. I literally contemplated going right there in a plastic cup. But God was listening to me that day as intently as I was listening to that man, and a break came up so that I could relieve myself and grab a pen and paper for instructions on what to do next.

When the program returned, the man who had been all up in my business before, came spookily into my house, not literally, but what he said next seemed like he had been in my home with me even before now. "You think you're waking up every morning to check the house, make sure the stove is off and check that the doors are locked?" he said.

I think I actually nodded in slow motion as if to say, "Yes. How did you know that?" I'm sure my mouth hung a little open at the timeliness of what was happening.

The man talking on the PBS station that night was internationally known author and speaker Dr. Wayne Dyer, known for his messages on self-development and spiritual growth.

Wayne warned that this in fact was "Jesus calling," my words not his. A literal attempt from God to spend time and tell me something important He had to say. Wayne went on to say it would take some effort to get your feet back on the floor now that we knew we were being invited to communion with God, even though we had eagerly got up without knowing what this really was. But if we would just put our feet on the ground every morning, about a week later our legs would activate and carry us to a comfortable place where we could get a download.

As he had explained, it would be a week before I took that familiar stroll through my house again. This time, I knew what it would be for. Finally, I summoned my feet to touch the floor. They directed me straight to the living room. Sitting on the couch, I listened. "I'm here, God," I spoke in my head. "I'm here to listen, but please don't speak. I will be terrified and I'm not ready for that." When I didn't hear Him say anything, I mumbled, "Thank God." I didn't really know how to talk to God. I didn't know what He sounded like, and I really didn't think I wanted that day to be the day I found out.

I reached underneath my coffee table for my Bible. It fell open to the book of Ephesians and I turned the pages until I got to chapter three, verse seventeen. At that moment, I had an encounter with God. "That Christ may dwell in your hearts by faith; that ye, being rooted and grounded in love, may be able to comprehend with all saints what is the breadth, and length, and depth, and height; and to know the love of Christ, which passeth knowledge, that ye might be filled with all the fulness of God" (Ephesians 3:17–19, KJV)

I also sought out the wisdom in 1 Corinthians 3:17 (KJV): "If any man defile the temple of God, him shall God destroy; for the temple of God is holy, which temple ye are."

While sitting there on our couch in the middle of the night, I got my first indication that God could see me.

From that night forward, every time I woke up, I would start reading at chapter three, verse seventeen of whatever book the Bible fell open to. The longer I did this, I had to start being intentional, because I had read so many other books, at that point. I would go to the book where I left off the previous morning or whatever books had a chapter three. I would read until it no longer applied to what I was going through in my life. After reading the Bible, I would write feverishly in the journal I kept about the things I was learning from Scripture, along with what God was telling me. I was so engrossed in reading the Bible and writing my thoughts that before I realized it, the sun would be peeking through that kitchen window, signaling it would soon be time for me to get my children ready for school.

God and I continued like that for weeks. I went through the entire Bible using that same approach—chapter three, verse seventeen— and read until it no longer applied to my circumstance. My search was aided by a study Bible that provided brief explanations of Scripture passages being read. It also offered supplemental or complementary passages to affirm where God said something similar at a different time.

I would go down the rabbit hole in search of an answer. Deep down on that trek through the night, I found more than an answer, I found The Answer, I found God. That time of searching Scripture passages while probing my thoughts was a turning point in my life. I learned to hear the voice of God at 3:17 a.m. During those dark hours every morning, I learned that God's voice doesn't necessarily have a sound, at least not one that you've heard before or that could be recognized as belonging to Him. But I know that God's voice, on that first late-night excursion, spoke to me using the voice of Wayne Dyer in that moment: "Don't go back to sleep."

I honestly believe that God takes over people's voices to get our attention. There have been many times that God's asked me, "Will you let me use your voice today? I need to speak through you to somebody else." God will use my voice or use someone else's voice to give another whatever they need.

Though you may not know it at the time, it comes in little whispers that suggest such things as "Read this passage before you leave home today. And then when you arrive at work, a girl in the office is in need of an answer that you had just read about earlier." Sometimes it comes from a conversation shared casually between two friends that enlightens the other on just exactly what needs to be done. Then other times God comes in the form of a PBS special in the middle of the night. Just when you thought it was time to go back to sleep, you get swept into a television program that would shift everything. At other times when God speaks, the message is meant precisely for you and nobody else.

Sometimes it is not to even be shared. As God was guiding me through this part of my journey, one of the last things I remember Him showing me was Deuteronomy 30:19 (NIV): "This day I call the heavens and the earth as witnesses against you that I have set before your life and death, blessings, and curses. Now choose life, so that you and your children may live."

I heard God's voice speak from the black-and-white print on the pages before me. "I have given you all kinds of businesses, Mignon." I had gotten a lot of veil orders after our wedding. Later, I customized books by covering them with unique or colorful fabric, something my mom had taught me how to do for photo albums, journals, Bibles, and things like that. Then I became a photographer, and now here I was embarking on a new journey. Each night with journal in hand I would write down thoughts that came to my head after reading. As the last night of being awakened began to approach, I had filled an entire spiral bound journal with the ideas I had garnered at 3:17 a.m.

I also knew I had to be faithful and follow His guidance to me. "Be careful to do what I have commanded. You just do exactly what I told you and do it how I told you to do it, and I will make you successful." Words like these appear throughout Scripture. We are to follow His leadership and His Word. "Keep this Book of the Law always on your lips; meditate on it day and night, so that you may be careful to do everything written in it. Then you will be prosperous and successful" (Joshua 1:8, NIV).

In that moment it was clear. God was looking for a return on His investment. I promised God in those dark hours, that if He would keep His promise of success to me, then I would tell anyone who would listen about what they could do if only they believed, and I have been on that mission ever since.

I asked God for something I could do to help my husband make ends meet.

I heard Him say, "Bake sale. Go make cupcakes."

Recipe Note to My Younger Self...

Stop watching other people live their lives and go create a story worth following.

Making It . . . from Scratch

S ince I didn't know much about baking, I approached our daughters, who loved baking. Their dad would direct them to make a box mix cake every day. At first, it was something for them to do, because we always loved having cake in our house. They had to learn what makes a "made from scratch" cake superior. They were constantly going back to the drawing board. What's the difference between a homemade cake and a box cake? How are the flavors different?"

I got an inspiration. "What if we made a business out of this?" I asked my daughters.

"That would be cool," they agreed.

As soon as they confirmed that they were interested in joining my little business venture, I went to one of our neighbors who owned a printing company and asked him to create the "Bakery Coming Soon" sign for the house.

Almost as soon as I ordered the sign, though, my oldest daughter, Lauren, let me know she really wasn't interested in my bakery idea. She was sixteen and had her sights on graduating from high school and all the activities associated with it. She had a plan for her own life, and it didn't have anything to do with my life plan. She was going back to New Orleans after graduation. Without Lauren, my younger daughter wasn't interested in sticking around either. That meant I had to learn the tools and tricks of how to bake. The sign I'd put outside let everybody know a bakery was coming soon. Since I had announced it to the entire world, I couldn't quit.

More than a bakery, though, I wanted what the people chatting with Ramsey on the radio were so excited about. I wanted that feeling. So I started working on my baking skills and soon I felt like everything I found on the Internet, every commercial, every television special, billboard, and magazine—everything was pointing toward "This is how you bake."

But I wanted the personal advice of someone with proven skills in the kitchen, someone I could trust, so I called my favorite baker. "Grandma, I need your help. The man on the radio says I could get out of debt by having a bake sale."

My grandmother, my father's adoptive mother, didn't know what I was talking about. All she remembered me talking about was becoming a doctor. "Why are you trying to have a bake sale? You don't even like being in the kitchen." She laughed and was genuinely perplexed at the same time.

"Grandma, I need help making your strawberry cake," I needed to stay on topic. My grandmother chuckled a lot at what she thought seemed foolishly ridiculous and confusing.

"Guh," she said, using the casual way my grandmother usually referred to me in her thick bayou accent meaning girl. I never remember her calling me by my name except when she was speaking about me, but rarely when she was speaking directly to me. "Grandma doesn't have recipes. I just pick up the ingredients in my hand."

But my grandmother, who has since passed away, was all in for me. She agreed to help me make her most sought-after cake over the phone, like we had done years before. My grandmother had long been my biggest fan, especially when it came to feeding me. That was her love language. "Chiiiiiile," she said. Her words paused as if to give space for her thoughts in between. Each word sang out a slow drawl. I could tell she was thinking about how to describe the amount of each ingredient needed to make her cake. She was effortless in the kitchen.

My grandmother never used measuring cups. She never gave a second thought to things like teaspoons. She moved quickly and slowly all at the same pace. After a moment of silence, she continued. "Open up your hand. You put that much flour in there, and then you know how you measure on your hand? You've got those little lines on your fingers? Well, I usually pick the first line on my finger for this, and I usually take the second line on my middle finger...." My grandmother was thoughtful about everything. Before we ended our conversation, she warned, "I don't know what you plan to do with this, but this is how I do it."

I wrote down everything she said like notes from school. My first stab at it wasn't that great. But not necessarily because I wasn't good at baking. At first, I thought it was because grandmothers, and I don't just mean mine, sometimes don't make the same cake twice. With a little pinch of this and a little bit of that, you might not ever be able to recreate what you love about what comes from her kitchen. Baking is a science, and if you don't have it right, you might make a mess or you might make a masterpiece. I think God was using that truth to show me that the success He promised me would require discipline. I couldn't do it my way; I had to do it His way. When I learned to follow rules, stick to them, and do it that way every time, things changed for the better.

I wrote the recipe out using exact measurements. If I was going to have a business doing this, it would have to be the same every single time. If the bakery was going to belong to me, I could use my grandmother's influence, but the recipe had to be mine.

I applied what I knew about science to Grandma's recipe. I took what she was calling measuring to the first line on my finger, and I made those teaspoons. I measured the scoop of my hand. I now know that my hand is a half cup. I kept testing it. When I got through, I was able to figure out what my grandmother meant.

When I first wrote down my grandmother's instructions during that afternoon call, it looked like scratch. I stared at the piece of white printer paper that I had scribbled notes all over. One-fourths, and two-thirds, and cups and teaspoons. I had made so many notes, but none of it made complete sense.

Look for the lesson, I thought, reading slowly and pacing my eyes left to right for a clue of what I might have missed. The cake looked like my grandmother's, sort of, but it didn't taste like it. There were lumps of what appeared to be unmixed flour that never got dissolved in the liquid of the batter. There were hunks of strawberries mixed in with the lumpy flour, making for a cake that was sort of hard or tough in sections.

"What in the world?" Brittany wondered aloud, coming over to taste it. She didn't want another bite. In fact, she didn't want to finish the bite she already had mid chew.

My initial thought was, "What could I do to this strawberry cake recipe so that it's mine?" Later I realized that I wasn't asking good questions of myself. The question really should have been "What can I do to make this cake good?" Honestly, if I couldn't get the cake recipe to good, then I didn't want it to be mine.

I was adamant, possibly even religiously so, about a of couple things when it came to the recipe. First, I understood and accepted that my strawberry cake was going to be different than my grandmother's. It had to be something I could replicate commercially—every single time. With a name like mine there would be no mistaking where this had come from. I needed the flavor to match the effort I had been putting in. If I was going to be the Beyoncé of baking, it had to taste fabulous. In finding my way to the kind of baker I wanted to be, I wanted to know the why behind the process and ingredients I was using. Why baking soda? Why baking powder? Why sometimes both? Why sometimes one? Can you use one if you don't have the other? Why self-rising flour? Why not? What the heck is cream of tartar? Isn't that for fish? Turns out cream of tartar has a couple of uses from cleaning to baking, can be substituted easily for things already in the kitchen, and is a chemical formula $KC_4H_5O_6$. Wait one second. I know this. This is chemistry.

When I was in college as a pre-med student, my roadblock was organic chemistry. I could not apply the science to the human body. I was clueless and left behind in the lab, trying to finish experiments that other students had long since mastered and moved on from. I would feel embarrassed, inadequate, and stupid. Eventually I gave up because I just thought I was incapable of balancing equations

Recipe Note to My Younger Self...

Nothing is wasted. Every stupid thing you've ever had to do is taking you from where you are to where you want to be. When you don't know the ultimate plan for your life, any route will take you there. So then, if you make a mistake, or a take a late turn, how do you know it wasn't already part of the plan. How do you know that it wasn't just necessary?

and writing empirical formulas. But here it was staring at me in my kitchen. Something seemed different now. In this form, it made all kinds of sense. The concept in my kitchen was chemical reactions that could be drilled down to their most basic parts.

Once I got an understanding of what it took to be successful at baking a particular product, I started tweaking ingredients. What would happen if I did this? What would happen if I changed that? Mainly I learned that if I knew the properties or characteristics of a substance, generally something else could accomplish the same result. I went to my husband, who knew his way around the kitchen well, for help. A few years prior, he had been accepted into the Culinary Institute of America. We had planned to move our family to New York to enroll him in school there, but with limited finances and a young family, relocating to New York from New Orleans was like moving to a land far, far away where the people spoke another language. He had already purchased the books before we resolved that we wouldn't be able to relocate affordably in a foreign place. He also had worked in a cafeteria and a restaurant so he knew some things about commercial cooking; he just wouldn't tell me.

"All my culinary books are in there. Go figure it out."

There it was again, things that seemed like they were wrong choices were proving to be part of the all-things-work-together-for-me plan.

"Fine," I thought. "Challenge accepted." Even more determined I learned every aspect of baking, and I started writing my own versions of recipes. Sometimes in the middle of the night, I shoveled warm pieces of cake in his half-asleep face from my kitchen laboratory. He never refused that sweet taste of sugar on his lips. His response was my cue whether it was ready for market testing.

For two years, more than seven hundred days, I worked every day on my business, as if the bakery was already open, as if my life depended on it. My life was depending on it. I had not forgotten what God had warned me in those early waking hours: "Choose life." And that's what I did, even when it seemed like He had forgotten me.

I talk a lot about the why, but what people really want to know is the how.

Baking is science. So then, I used the scientific method approach to create a successful recipe and brand. There are five steps to the scientific method.

1. *Define a problem*. I need to find a way to get out of debt and help make ends meet for my family.

2. *Make a prediction from observations*. People are getting out of debt by having bake sales.

3. *Ask questions, conduct experiments, and gather data*. What if I could have a bake sale every single day? Test your ingredients and know your why.

4. *Analyze the data and form a hypothesis*. Made-from-scratch recipes take people back to a nostalgic place where they experienced something created with love. People will come from miles around for the memories.

5. *Draw a conclusion*. Write an award-winning recipe and sell the resulting product for profit.

In other words, essentially this is what I was doing. I prayed for something I could do. God answered and said make cupcakes. I played with ingredients in the kitchen tweaking ingredients to create my own version of my favorite dessert, cake. I planned my business model waking up in the wee hours of the morning and talking to God about what He wanted for me. I prepared for the opportunity. They say success is discovered at the intersection of preparation and opportunity. Let's say I changed my address and moved to that location so I wouldn't miss a thing.

Our historic neighborhood had a lot of up-and-coming new residents, but in those days, it was still considered the "hood." Some people were afraid to open the door when I appeared unannounced, offering something I had baked at home. Many assumed I was at their door to beg for something rather than to welcome them to the neighborhood with cupcakes. In this transactional culture we live in, most probably feared I would say, "Oh, now you owe me because I gave you something." I wanted to be good enough with no strings attached. It was never too hard a sale once I told them that I was the lady from the bakery house with the sign that read "coming soon."

After moving toward the gathering data phase, my market research consisted of looking out of the two eight-foot windows in the front of our home to spot realtors showing properties that had just been built across the street. When we moved here, ours was mostly a mixed-use neighborhood with industrial plants and warehouses sprinkled between cottages and flanked by larger executive homes. When I saw people in the neighborhood looking at houses, I would walk up to them and say, "Excuse me, I'm the one with the house that says, 'Bakery Coming Soon,' and I'm working on a new recipe. I want to know if you would try something I'm working on."

They would actually do it. And happily. Their response was, "I mean, who doesn't want free cupcakes?" Thereafter, those people would knock on my door asking for more. Sometimes they'd even offer me money on the sidewalk to take whatever extra I had left.

One of my early successes in Germantown was a mini lemon drop cupcake that I bathed in a coating of icing sugar and lemon juice. Led by the leader of lemon lovers, a.k.a. my neighbor Joanie, I sold them in small batches to real estate agents, people who were buying homes in the neighborhood, and the people already living there.

The nature of our Germantown community was quite possibly a major reason for my success. At the same time, it's also the very reason people thought it would never work.

"Poor girl is clueless," one neighbor shared after having supported the business for more than fifteen years. They really believed no one was coming to Germantown to stand in line for anything, let alone gourmet, and certainly not cupcakes.

Oh, how wrong they were. Guess they underestimated the wrong cupcake!

Still unaware of the turmoil we were experiencing as a family, Joanie became a mouthpiece for me, selling others on why they should try the lemon ones even if they vowed that they didn't eat cupcakes. She would tell other neighbors, "Have you tasted what Mignon is making?"

The people in that community liked and supported one another. We had chili cook-offs and garden guzzles, which were essentially excuses to go from house to house and check out the interior of our neighbors' homes, drink their beer, eat their food, and go on to the next. It was eat-and-run at its best. When the word got out about the girl in the purple house, people started using that patinaed pineapple like it was the secret handshake into the cupcake club.

From asking for things I didn't even have on my radar to baking a piece of their family history, my neighbors and friends pushed me beyond what I knew I could do. I tested the heat conduction of different metals and ordered pans from around the globe. My passion to succeed sent me back into that house for weeks at a time, pushing out product like they were hits on the radio. I guess you could say, I was baking hits.

That's how I started building a following. My cupcakes were slowly becoming the neighborhood buzz, and it now had a name that the neighbors were beginning to share—The Cupcake Collection. Mainly what began as a gesture to offer a bit of sweetness to newcomers, came back to me like dividends that had gained interest.

I was learning to become what I needed to become. I didn't know I was building a brand. I didn't know I was making something that people wanted to follow. I didn't know that millions would be trying to figure out how to do what I was doing.

Here's what I had going for me.

First, the neighborhood restaurants introduced me to their clients. The Mad Platter restaurant asked me to make cupcakes for their Thursday morning meetups. That put me in front of a lot of decision makers who wanted to take them back as quickly as they discovered them. Monell's, an extremely popular family-style restaurant, allowed my son to pass out fliers to the crowds waiting for tables and even added the cupcakes to the end of the meal for sampling during dessert. I can't begin to count the many friends we have met coming over to The Cupcake Collection for dessert after eating at Monell's.

Second, people buy from people they know. We were members of the neighborhood and were just as vested with our neighbors as they were with us. Our daughter was the resident babysitter and the few kids that lived near us loved her.

Third, if you take care of me, when the opportunity arises, I'll take care of you. A couple who lived across the field from our house was expecting a baby, and late one night an unexpected knock sent me into the kitchen long after my bedtime had passed.

"My wife is craving. Do you have anything in there?" A tired and hopeful young husband stood on my porch at 10:00 p.m., combing his fingers through thick black hair.

"Yes, red velvet, right?' I remembered him. This wasn't the first time, and having experienced it personally, I understood how pregnancy cravings hit—fast, intrusive, and unexpected—so I stayed ready for her most times. I packaged the few I had for him, and he took them back across the field. That was what got them through their cravings at night.

My cupcakes were becoming a thing. But it was an encounter I had with a stranger at my door early one morning that would take me by surprise. I was getting used to the intrusive knocking sound of the brass pineapple, and by this time, the requests no longer shocked me. Except this time, there really wasn't a request, but more like a demand for action.

When I answered the door, a lady I'd never seen before was standing there wearing a nice outfit accessorized with a little attitude.

"I came to let you know that your 'Bakery Coming Soon' sign is a lie," she said, "and you need to take it down off your house."

Confused and unsure I had heard her correctly, I just stared, waiting for some clarity as to why this woman I didn't know had an issue with my sign. She needed to vent her frustration at the source. She was there to reprimand me for how long it was taking me to get the place open.

"I know when you put that sign up there because I have been driving by here every day for the last two years waiting for this bakery that's never coming. I need you to know that it's a lie. Your bakery's never coming soon."

"What's your favorite kind of cake?" I replied calmly after letting her vent. I really hadn't considered the fact that people were actually paying attention to the sign and waiting for me to open.

"Red velvet."

"What time do you get off work?"

"Five o'clock."

"Come by then."

She and her best friend came back to the house after work, and I invited them in. We sat and ate red velvet cupcakes in my living room, where I had invited them in to try what I had made for them. While they were at work, I had gone to the store and bought ingredients specifically to make red velvet cupcakes for them, not sure if they would even come back. But I needed every deal and every touch point to land on a return customer. That's exactly what they became—regular customers from that day. They started taking cupcakes to their office. They detoured by our house every week to see if the bakery was open yet. It wasn't open officially, but that didn't stop them from coming by. They faithfully placed orders and brought new business with them.

I constantly told myself that I could be sick or I could be tired. I didn't have the luxury of being both.

God allowed me to go through those days to sharpen me, so that when I came into larger spaces, no one could break me and tell me I wasn't good enough because I did my work to be in that space, and I know I'm the best.

I have watched other businesses that look like mine open ahead of mine and then close while we remain open. I'm the last cupcake man standing. It's because all the pain that I had been through, the waiting, the turmoil, and the tears that I had to cry, watching them beat me to the finish line, and sometimes laugh in my face about it, made me a strong survivor.

"There's Room for More Cupcakes"

"You can't see the picture when you're in the frame."
~ Les Brown

That's such an apt metaphor for my life, and that's also what got me through that season of my life. As excited as I was for my cupcakes to be gaining popularity, I still didn't know exactly what I was doing. What's more, I didn't know how to move my life forward. I was just surviving, and baking cupcakes was the way I'd found to do it. I didn't know where I was heading, but God knew. So, every day, while I was in survival mode, I was building the foundations for a life.

I had been baking cupcakes by the order out of my converted living room for about two years, like it was a job, trying to get my bakery open, when it happened. Somewhere in that timeframe, I was driving down the street with five-year-old Xavier in tow and I saw a sign that made me slam the brakes. There, in the middle of Division Street, a fairly busy corridor to downtown Nashville, hung a white banner with pink lettering above a whimsical awning proclaiming the news, "GiGi's Cupcakes Coming Soon."

"God, how is it that I'm working every day to make this happen and you let this bakery open before mine?" Real tears streamed down my face. Xavier, seated behind me in his car seat, tapped me on the shoulder, trying to comfort me. "Mommy, just because she's first doesn't mean she'll be the best."

"Okay." I took my foot off the brakes and turned the corner. The tears wouldn't stop, though, so I stopped the car again.

"Mommy, we have to move," his tiny voice suggested. I didn't answer. There was just a moment of silence while I sat and stared at it. Then, that little, tiny voice spoke big wisdom. "Don't be sad, Mommy. There's room for more cupcakes."

I couldn't believe how wise my baby was. I have lived by his words ever since that day, "There's room for more cupcakes." It took a five-year-old to teach me that there was room for GiGi to sell cupcakes on that side of town, and room for my bakery on our side of town.

I had hopes and dreams, but I honestly had no idea what was going on with my life. God did. After two years, I was frustrated that I still hadn't managed to get the bakery open. What I didn't know then was that everything I was going through in that time of my life was preparing me to become a successful entrepreneur. Had I not been sitting at the back of my house, studying what I was going to be doing next, on the day Joanie came over wanting to buy six hundred

Recipe Note to Self...

Blessings don't warn you that they're coming. "If you stay ready, you don't have to get ready."

cupcakes, and if I hadn't answered the door in obedience, and had I not begun to figure out what it was going to take to make baked goods sell, to bake things people would want to eat and to practice, practice, practice my craft, I wouldn't have been ready to receive what God was about to do for me.

During that period when God was waking me at 3:17 in the morning, I understood that life was being offered to me and that I had a choice to make—I could choose life, or I could choose death. I wanted to live, and I wanted to live fully. I always knew something special was supposed to happen for me. I always knew I was supposed to accomplish something, to be something in the world. But I didn't know what and I didn't know when.

What I could see in those wandering days was that had I not done the work of becoming noticeable and recognizable with the product to the point where my neighbor would knock on the door and say, "Can you make more of these?" I would have missed an open door. Or had I not said yes to her, despite us having no electricity, all factors would not have been aligned for me to receive the blessing God had in store for me. My blessing gave me no warning; it seemed to come out of nowhere.

But some of the best blessings come as calls to action. God would take care of me and He knew what He had in store for me, but I needed to take what He brought to my door and turn it into action.

Joanie's visit had been a blessing, although she could not have known what it would take for me to fill her order. She had unwittingly asked me to take my family's last five dollars and make cupcakes with it. She couldn't have known how we were really living, hand to mouth. To put her blessing into action, I needed to move, but I still wasn't sure how—because living how and where we were could be discouraging to anyone struggling to fit in and make ends meet. All the work I had put in so far was a foundation, but I still lack the courage to build the rest of it.

We were in an up-and-coming neighborhood. A community that had been known as the "hood" was evolving into an affluent neighborhood. But all I could see looking around was how everybody else seemed to be making it, and I wasn't. As I walked through the neighborhood, looking at what my neighbors had, all I kept thinking was, "God what do they have that I don't? Do you love them more than me?"

The lyrics to "Otis," a tribute song to Otis Redding, performed by Kanye West and Jay-Z, popped in my head. It was the part about having multiple luxury vehicles.

The lyrics cut into me.

"Seriously, God? They have options and they're all luxurious, and I still don't have anything." The lyrics prompted me to have a quick chat with God. As I walked through the neighborhood, looking at what my neighbors had accumulated, all I kept thinking was, "God, what do they have that I don't, that they have all this. Do you love them more than me?" I had already believed that my earthly father didn't love me, so I think I expected the same from my heavenly one too. But I heard something different in that walk with God.

"Are you willing to do what they do, to get what they have?" God asked me.

"Ouch! I felt that, God."

"Are you willing to put in what she puts in to get what she gets in return?"

I realized that I couldn't recall a lot of successful people, except maybe Dave Ramsey and a couple of others, who talked in great detail about how hard their journey was. Still, among those testimonies I was familiar with, I never heard one successful person say, "Oh, I would never go back through that again." Successful people don't usually say, "It cost me too much to get to where I am." They recognize that the mental, emotional, spiritual, and physical price cost was the price of admission into their arena of success.

But I knew what God was saying to me. I knew what I had to do. I understood that success meant that work and sacrifice were required of me. I also knew that even though it was going to be hard, I would be able to do it.

I determined that I wanted something big from God. That I wanted to do what I had seen Beyoncé do in music—but in baking. I wanted to be like Lil' Wayne with my wedding cakes.

That's when I started studying their hustle. If they could be the best performers, become famous, and make billions, why couldn't I be great, too? And I knew people who are incredibly successful did not have an easy journey. A lot of those people whose success I wanted to emulate had come from backgrounds similar to mine—people who were wildly successful stayed up all night; I had been doing that. They sometimes locked themselves away for extended periods to create an end product for the world to enjoy; I had been doing that, too.

I was willing to work on my dream in the dark. I was willing to skip French fries and fun for now, to get the things I needed to make my name great. We ate red beans and rice for weeks. We were eating potatoes and cheese for a chance at being successful.

But what was God asking me that I wasn't already doing? What was he challenging me to change?

I couldn't stop with lyrics; I had to look for the lifestyle and I had to look to their lives for lessons. I found some commonalities in the most successful people that I could use to build my brand:

Quit quitting. What I found from the people I wanted most to be like was that they worked hard until they achieved what they were after. They were not quitters. I was a quitter. The first step in being successful is to actually quit quitting on yourself.

Be regimented. Every person I watched led a disciplined life of some sort. They lived within confines that didn't imprison them, but those boundaries were havens that kept them, their craft, their gift optimal and safe.

Practice your craft. Hours and hours were put in, and they never complained about being tired. They never complained that it was hard. But what I've learned in my own journey is that you can't advance yourself or the kingdom if you're tired. You can be better after rest.

Get rest. While they were working, they might pull long hours, but when the assignment is over, they retreat from the public eye and take an absence from interviews because they are rejuvenating and getting ready for the next great thing. What I learned is that work without rest is a recipe for failure.

Finally...

Believe in you. Not one of those wildly successful icons I studied had to be convinced that they were great, let alone good enough. Practice proved that for them. They believed in themselves when nobody else did. People won't always be cheering for you so you have to cheer sometimes for yourself.

That's the kind of stuff that God and I talked about. If I wanted to be the best, I knew I had to work out how to get there. I wanted to make my name great for my family, and I was willing to tell people that it wasn't me. It was God. It was all His idea. I began asking myself and God, "What is it going to take to be Beyoncé in baking?"

Behind the scenes people started calling me "Mignoncé" and the name started to stick. All I needed now was to enlarge my platform so that the world could "Taste and see that the Lord is good." In the words of Beyoncé, "This is so much bigger!"

I knew I had a lot of work to do, but hard work was as familiar to me as old shoes. I had done it all my life, starting in my teens.

Decisions, Decisions

When my husband and I made the decision to put our
energies into making The Cupcake Collection a bona
fide business, it was also a decision to get a divorce.

The day we decided to pursue the degree in earnest should have
been one of the happiest days of my life, but I was in a really broken
space. My husband said he wanted a divorce, and although I agreed
we needed to part ways, I had reservations.

"How are you going to leave me when I raised your children?
My whole life has been supporting your businesses and raising our
family, and now you want to leave? What am I supposed to do?"

"Why don't you just leave? You have a college degree," he said.

"How can I leave? I haven't done anything with it because I
have been raising these children, our children. I have nothing."

"Well, fine. Let's get the bakery open." Silence followed that
seemed like an eternity. Okay! That's the decision!

Opening the bakery required money that I couldn't source from
conventional means. We barely had what it took to run our house, let
alone throwing in the extra costs of building a business. So, in the

fashion of insanity, I did what I had always done before expecting a different result. Back to work I went, intending to earn money I could wield for the bakery to be built. Around that time, revisiting the opportunity I discovered at FedEx, I thought a package handler job would get me what I needed. I could work in the warehouse overnight or very early in the morning while my family was asleep or before they would wake up. When I applied for a job at UPS, the hiring manager, who was extremely nice to me, wondered if I was sure that this was the type of job that I wanted to do. I was sure. I took an assessment and after I passed the test, I made sure that my phone would be on to get the call back. I went home and made cupcakes.

François wasn't fond of me working in this way. Sitting at the table with those cupcakes, he convinced me that a better use of my time would be to use the four hours I would spend throwing packages around on building my business. "If you'll be serious about this baking thing you want to do, I'll give you my man cave."

He had a room in our home that was dedicated to all things Alvin François. It was a living room where he had installed a big projector screen on the wall that was essentially off limits. The kids weren't allowed to really go in there except to watch movies, and then only with their dad's permission. He had a pool table on the other side of the room, and it was all decorated with him in mind. He said, "You can do it right here in our house. You don't have to go anywhere."

I remember being disappointed at the prospect. When we started looking for locations for my bakery, we quickly discovered that we couldn't afford anything. I'd waited so long to actually open a business that doing it from our home wasn't what I had envisioned. Still, I was grateful to have space I could use.

Something seemed so right about that, even though I was too shy to market myself like I had seen him do. Maybe I just had not been hungry enough.

*"When you want to success as bad as you want to breathe,
then you'll be successful."*

~ Dr. Eric Thomas, the Hip Hop Preacher

I did want to be successful and staying here following the same old thing took my air. I had felt poverty's pinch with him, but what would I do alone with no one to navigate with? But I was sick and tired of being sick and tired and decided to show up for me. I was hungry enough.

"All right, I can do this here."

When they called me about the job, I went to the hiring office for preliminary paperwork with cupcakes in tow. Even though I needed the income from that job, I had a change of heart. "Thank you," I told the UPS hiring manager, "but I don't think I'm going to accept the job. I'm going to open a cupcake bakery."

With a jovial smile that seemed genuinely impressed and excited, the manager wished me luck, made sure that I was indeed sure that I was making the decision I thought was best, and then promised to come and patronize my business when I got it open.

That was the day that everything changed. I was stepping further out on faith than I had before. As far as I was out in here in the deep, I was going to have to keep my eyes on Jesus. This was going to be sink or swim.

Our neighborhood and our house were already zoned mixed use, which meant we could operate a business and live in the same place. It even had a separate entrance, a feature that would make it simpler to get my bakery business approved in our residence.

Back when we were renovating the house, I'd found a door in an antique junkyard that I loved. The door, which looked as though it had been the entrance to a store in its former life, had a glass window trimmed in a wide flat wood border all around. In our home we made it stationary, so it served a purely aesthetic purpose. When

The Cupcake Collection was about to open, I prepped that door for all the people who would push upon her frame. I puttied, sanded, bonded, and painted it like new to be the front door to the bakery. Everything for the bakery was housed in that man cave for cupcakes.

My husband had one condition for giving up his space for The Cupcake Collection. I could not paint the ceiling. He had worked so hard to faux paint it. The beautiful copper ceiling was the result of a three-step process that he did, lying on his back on a scaffold that he had built to reach the thirteen-foot ceilings.

I went to a supply store with a swatch of the color. The woman working in the paint department had already been working with us on our house, helping us pick out paint themes. She selected an orange color that she thought would complement the ceiling. At first, I wasn't convinced. She persuaded me to go home and give it a try. I did know something about color and now this lady had my interest piqued. I knew I wanted to be taken seriously and pink cupcakes were for play in my mind, but now I gave a second thought to my brand. I had studied brands and color in college. When I was about to graduate, I wrote a thesis on the psychology of color in branding. (Little did I know God was setting me up for what I would need to know in the future about my own brand.)

That orange became the signature color of The Cupcake Collection. Orange seemed perfect. It is the color of happiness and joy. People trust things that are orange, I thought. I wanted to be so intentional about spreading happiness that customers would feel it when they came inside. They might come in feeling down and wouldn't know why they felt happy by the time they left. I knew. I had picked the color of joy, painted it all over the walls, and put in the logo and branding so that they would be surrounded by a warming welcome into my home.

I started with a dorm-sized refrigerator—that was all I needed to pass inspection—and a Kitchen-Aid mixer. Using the house for the business location was a blessing I hadn't seen coming. The cost of doing business there, with such low overhead, saved on the bottom line in the beginning, when sales were essentially nonexistent. Plus, making it there killed two birds with one stone. We were able to pay for a place to live and provide a place for my business to thrive at the same time.

Recipe Note to Self...

All you have is all you need to get started on the journey. Today, you have everything you need to be successful for where you are for today. Check out what Jesus says in Matthew 6:34. Tomorrow will take care of itself.

At first, I thought I would need so much more to successfully open a bakery—a large commercial refrigerator, or several for that matter, lots of mixers filling up a room that was big enough for baking, along with several convection ovens to boot. But I didn't need those on day one.

We had bought a three-compartment sink from a yard sale and shopped on Craigslist for deals on equipment. We bartered, paying plumbers and other tradesmen with products or services. My husband would go to their house and barter deals to do work in exchange for services on ours. "I'm going to fix this for you. I'll come and give you _____, in exchange for you doing the work at the bakery." That's how we did things differently. We stayed out of debt and we had turned a bake sale into a business.

"Do you remember me?" a man I didn't know asked, flashing his glowing smile. He had stopped me the morning I was on the way into a board meeting at Lipscomb University where I serve as an advisor to the college of business.

"I know your face, but I don't know why," I told him.

"I was the manager who was going to hire you at UPS," he reminded me, "and you said, 'No, I think I'm going to open my business.'"

Gleason Rodgers had remembered that encounter and he kept his word to buy cupcakes, not only once, but many times since.

Choose Life

When God was waking me up at 3:17 every morning to tell me what He wanted me to do—that He was setting before me life and death, that He was giving me one more time, one more chance to follow in the purpose that He had given me, that He wanted me to tell other people about what He had done for me so that they could believe they can do it too—I promised God if He would make me successful, I would tell anyone who would listen about what they could do if they believe.

God was waking me every morning at the same time to collaborate with me, to tell me the idea, to give me the ammunition to get started. What He told me in those hours, I learned in the Book of Deuteronomy 30:19 (NIV): "This day I call the heavens and the earth as witnesses against you that I have set before you life and death, blessings, and curses. Now choose life, so that you and your children may live."

"Choose life, Mignon." I believe that God was saying, "Listen, I didn't send my Son for you to live in mediocrity. I sent Him so that you would live, choose to live, choose to be a light to other people so that they can know what they can also do if they believe."

When we opened the bakery on November 9, 2008, we were slated to lose our home to foreclosure within the next thirty to forty-five days. I opened anyway, believing if God is who He says He is then He can do what He says He can do. A dorm-sized refrigerator and a Kitchen-Aid mixer were all the equipment I had to present on the day the health inspector came to grant me an occupancy license.

I had a ventless convection oven that, when filled to capacity, could hold one hundred and twenty cupcakes at a time. There were speed racks for cooling cupcakes and a three-compartment sink we had picked up and installed from a salvage yard for four hundred dollars. Thinking I needed to have big-time commercial equipment to get approval to open was so far off base. As he went through what was my husband's man cave converted for baking cupcakes, he pulled out a pad and silently marked off boxes. We had been on their roster for two years now, and the inspector was coming by to check on our progress and see if they could help move us along in the completion process.

"Do you think you can fit all of the ingredients you'll need to run your business in this refrigerator?" he asked, referring to the discarded dorm refrigerator my son had painted red to match his dorm décor. I had been using it to store butter and milk separately for my orders.

"I'd have to buy ingredients more often, but I can manage until things get busier," I told him as he tested the temperature on the inside.

"This will be just fine," he noted, giving the nod for my business to move forward.

After checking a few other things, he wrote a final remark on his yellow legal pad and handed me something to sign. When he was done, he handed the form back to me.

My eyes widened, not quite sure of what he had given me even though it looked like something official had just been accomplished.

"Open as soon as you like," he told me, giving The Cupcake Collection a passing score for opening day that was just shy of perfection. The inspector shook my hand and left the building.

We wasted no time celebrating. We had been working so hard to get the place going that we had forgotten we were heading our separate ways, or at least I had.

The diligent work it takes to start a new business kept François and me together, or perhaps kept me too preoccupied to notice. It would be seven years later—after two additional store locations, the introduction of Nashville's first dessert truck, one of only two food trucks in the city at that time, and a pop-up store—before we ever parted ways.

Whatever I Got, God Sent It

I **believe all my success has been and continues to be predicated** on following my spirit, as I am led by God. We chose November 9, 2008, as our opening day, believing God for something big. We needed more than money. We needed a miracle. We had landed on the foreclosure list and our property was being auctioned for sale the next month in December. Nevertheless, we opened believing that if God chose to, He could change things.

The night before we opened, my husband said, "We'll tell everybody we're going to open on Sunday. Go to bed, and when you wake up in the morning, it's going to be ready."

They sent me to bed because I needed to get up early to work. My kids and my husband worked on the finishing touches, and sure enough, when I woke up that morning, I had a bakery. The room was painted, and I had a counter. I didn't have a cash register, but I had a little adding machine.

I got up before three o'clock that morning to start preparing everything because all I had was the Kitchen-Aid mixer, a small oven, and a couple of shelves. I had to prepare many small batches. It would take me a while to bake everything.

That morning, when I got ready to open, my kids came up to me, hiding something behind their backs. They were so proud of me. "Mom, we have a gift for you," they announced. They pulled out a pickle jar that they had painted to say, "Tips." They explained, "We want people to give you tips for your hard work."

I was so moved by their thoughtfulness, I cried. Then I made them a deal. "I tell you what. Whenever anybody puts money in this tip jar, you can have it….if you come here and help me wash dishes and clean up. This will be your payment."

On opening day, all my friends came, church members came, and neighbors came. We had made little flyers on orange cardstock paper, and my kids had handed them out to people passing by. They waved at people to come in. We had a good first day. We sold everything we had. We assumed they would just come back and buy more. They didn't. People tell you they're going to come back, and they really do mean that. But sometimes they don't remember. Despite the initial enthusiasm at first, business did not take off right away. We started with a bang, and customers were telling others about The Cupcake Collection, and they were excited about it, too. Then they must have forgotten about it.

In the early days, I worked the bakery solo until my children came home from school to help clean. I sat there alone in a chair for what seemed like hours. All the side work chores and cleaning had been done without much interruption. I perched myself on the padded red dining chair that I had upholstered in an attempt to make classy chairs for my dining table. I had pulled one into the bakery and set it up against the wall under the phone that hung there. I was anticipating the phone ringing for sales, so when it did, I was happy. It was my husband calling to ask me how things were going.

I was sitting in the bakery, alone with no customers, and I had just counted the money in the moments before he called. I had made seventeen dollars that day. I let out a sigh as I settled my back into the chair. I opened my mouth to start complaining. "All I made today was seventeen dollars. I don't know...."

I stopped myself mid-sentence. I heard the Holy Spirit inside me say, "That seventeen dollars wasn't a surprise to God." He knew what He was sending me and that everybody coming there was being sent. They were being told. They didn't come by happenstance. They found my bakery because God sent them there. I made up in my mind that's what it was and that whether I got seventeen dollars or ten dollars, or whatever it was, God knew what was going on. I had to leave it to Him because I was in it only because He told me to be there.

"It's going okay. Whatever I got, God sent it," I told him. I had changed up my whole perspective from "All I got" to "Guess what God gave me?" My husband promised to come home soon so that I wouldn't be left there alone, and we hung up.

I never had another seventeen-dollar day. When I learned that I only needed to obey and show up, God started blessing me. I started having fifty-dollar days. I still remember my first one-hundred-dollar day. I never turned back.

That's how it took off. The day that I recognized that whatever came my way, God had given it to me. I didn't do anything different. The people would come by and see the bakery sign and buy cupcakes. They would go and tell somebody, "Y'all, I just had the best cupcakes I have ever had in my life."

People who worked nearby would stop in. One of the managers of a nearby office was allergic to everything in my building, but she wanted me to succeed. She would buy cupcakes for all her colleagues.

I would have a line down the block of customers waiting to get in soon. Once people tasted them, they would come back and tell other people. I always say if you could pay for word-of-mouth advertising, it would be worth whatever it costs.

Dead Silent

A house alive with energy and electricity has a hum. The clocks tick and music beats around every corner. Conversely, the sound of current ceasing to flow sends out a letdown reminiscent of air being released from a tire, only louder, faster, and more chilling. The sound that follows is dead silence.

We were familiar with both.

It's one thing to be sitting in your own darkness and trying to figure things out, and a whole other scenario when you have your first crowd in the room for cupcakes on a busy afternoon and the power company's cherry picker rolls up out front.

At 1213 6th Avenue North, we were no strangers to having our electric service disconnected. We had been cut off so many times that once we got our act together, Nashville Electric Service had to replace the connections that run from the pole to our home. I don't think those are meant for connecting and reconnecting regularly.

The word was out that we had cupcakes. Monell's, a family-style restaurant hotspot, located just a few houses up the block from ours, was hopping for lunch. The lunch crowd then made its way up our stairs and into my bakery for cupcakes. My first line! My husband grabbed an apron, and my son Alex was manning the crowd.

Our joy switched to panic when I turned my husband's attention to the eight-foot windows that frame the front of our cottage. We signaled to Alex what was happening and headed out the back door to beg for mercy.

Out back, we met two Nashville Electric Service workers who had just pulled into the alley behind our house. We knew what would happen next if he lifted that cherry picker into the air.

"Please don't let him shut my lights off." I prayed to God and pleaded with my husband to do something about what was happening. I would be so embarrassed if the lights went out with all those customers inside. My mind immediately went to if-this-then-that scenarios.

As François approached the back fence, I hopped on the phone and called for a lifeline.

Now was no time for niceties. "Mom, I need your help." I started spewing out numbers and details about a booming business I had made from scratch that was operating in my living room and my mother had not even a clue about it. I sold her in those moments about needing an investment and why it was a sure bet for her. I needed two thousand dollars wired to NES within thirty minutes or I was going to lose what I worked so hard for.

My mom had been done with lending us money for years now. Ever since the house in metro Atlanta, she had kept her distance financially. There was a pregnant pause and I waited for the questions.

"What's the account number?" As I was pleading my case to her, she had been writing down all the details. With no further questions, Mom became my angel investor.

The NES workers had given us thirty minutes to raise the money for the past due bill before they would be back to shut off service. They coordinated a signal for the receipt to be rolled up in the chain link. When they got there, they found a receipt and cupcakes courtesy of Mom, who was hundreds of miles away.

She didn't stay away for long, though. She was headed to Nashville on the next available flight to see "what in the Sam Hill was going on." That's about as harshly as she ever did speak.

Recipe Note to Self...

Ask and it shall be given, seek and you will find, knock and the door will be opened to you when you seek with the right intentions.

Phone a Friend

We tried everything possible to keep our purple house with the pineapple on the door. We had refinanced from Tim after year one just as we were closing business dealings. But the economy was rough, and he wasn't in the business of home mortgage lending. So we took an adjustable rate mortgage (ARM) with a company that skyrocketed our mortgage from $1,100 to more than $2,200 in a matter of weeks.

We signed all of the documents, and with our credit and money being in no better shape than we had been from the start, we were lucky to be getting a loan at all. Unable to make the new payments, our mortgage went up again, this time to more than $3,000 per month. We hadn't been able to pay $2,200 for the last nine months, much less paying anything toward the principal. We were struggling to keep the lights on and the water running, mainly because construction jobs had become scarce. Certified letters began rolling in when we heard that the Obama Administration was planning to enact legislation to help people like us who were caught up in the predatory lending trap.

In the meantime, I continued to shop for mortgage deals, despite getting turned down everywhere. By that point, because the neighborhood had transformed from the "hood" to a highly desirable location, we were worth more in foreclosure. We owed less than $200,000 on a house now worth four times that much. And because we were desperate, we couldn't get anyone to buy that quickly even had we been willing to sell it. Not sure what to do and facing foreclosure and losing yet another home that we had worked so hard to obtain, I went back to my knees in search of God and answers.

Our home was shaping up really well. The gold arch above the fifty-foot hallway was now backlit for the kids to use as a nightlight. Twelve feet of bricks, floor to ceiling, formed a herringbone pattern through the hall. A projector screen hung in the living room and a pool table flanked the east side of the room where the kids played on refurbished floors. Brittany's room was bubblegum pink and had a wainscoted reading nook with bookshelves for her Junie B. Jones collection.

The sights and sounds of home had consumed each of the rooms and the feeling of panic was filling my heart. I began to brace for insanity to show up again, so I did what I knew. While on my knees, I got the idea to make a call to the radio show. I figured Dave Ramsey would know what to do to help me save our home, if there were any possibilities.

I made the decision to call Dave Ramsey because I needed to understand my options.

"888-525-5225."

I heard the announcer call out the toll-free number as he indicated that live call lines were open. I picked up the phone, knowing I was unsure I really wanted to go through with this. What would Dave say? Would he tell me my debt was dumb? It was like waiting for my dad to come home when I had done something wrong.

I was further crippled by the fact that the first thing he would say is, "Caller, what's your name?" and then announce where I was calling from. I reconciled within myself that if anybody I knew was listening, they would know it was me and that I was losing my house. But just as quickly, I reasoned that whoever might be listening was in no way helping matters around here and that I had better tuck my tail and take whatever advice I could get no matter who might hear it. Worst case scenario—our foreclosure scenario helps someone else.

I swallowed my pride and dialed up the show. I got in on the first try. The phone rang and rang, and a producer who sounded like he was in a holding room answered my call and screened it for the show. After answering several questions about what kind of business I wanted to take up with Dave, they queued me for the call. "You'll be on next, right after this commercial."

I was nervous and happy and hopeful and scared as I waited for the call to commence. Dave Ramsey announced my name and he shared a little background on my story and why I was calling. The call was nothing like I had anticipated or feared. It was like talking to a father but not an angry one. This was a talk with a parent who had compassion, who understood that you had gotten yourself in hot water that you couldn't figure out on your own how to turn the heat down on. Dave had compassion, but his talk was frank. He explained my serious situation and flat out told me the lenders were trying to steal our house from us. That thought had occurred to me, but because we didn't have enough money coming in, were living way above our means and about to lose everything, including the cars we were driving, I thought we couldn't fight back. I thought they could do what they wanted to our property and our possessions.

For a moment, I forgot Whose I was.

Dave placed me on hold and promised to get my info during the break. When the show cut for commercial, a caring, fatherly voice assured me that even though the show was over, my dog in the fight with him wasn't done. Dave assigned his right-hand man to my case and things started looking up.

For weeks they stayed with me, checking and calling and pounding the pavement on our behalf when the final call came. "I'm so sorry, Mignon. We've done all we can do. These people want to take your house and that's what they are going to do." He further offered that his best advice was for us to have a short sale and cut our losses.

We began meeting with potential buyers and then one day something happened that we weren't prepared for.

Heading over to Sweet City, USA, the bakery supply house, to pick up decorations for cakes, a call came through my cell phone that changed everything. The mortgage lender had, without reason, decided to cease their pursuit of our foreclosure.

"What can you pay as a monthly note?" the lending agent's representative asked. Stunned, I told them what we could realistically pay, and they said the documents we needed to sign confirming the lower mortgage payment would be in the mail the following day.

There, right there on the asphalt in front of Sweet City, USA, we cried like babies because God himself had come to our rescue.

Recipe Note to Self...

It never goes the way you planned it in your head. Cast out fear and keep moving forward in faith to defeat the giant. God is able to do exceedingly abundantly above all you can ask or think!

You Can't Help a Chicken Hatch

Struggle pays dividends.

I **read somewhere that if you help a chicken hatch, it will die. If** a chicken is trying to hatch and you say, "Oh, let me help it," you're doing the chick a disservice. You can't help a chicken hatch. It's the adversity that the baby bird goes through, extricating itself from the eggshell, that makes the chicken strong enough to thrive. I feel as if that's been my life. The adversity that I had to go through made this chicken thrive and live strong.

Somewhere along the line I finally understood the adversity I had to go through allowed me to see that God had more in store for me than I even had the capacity to ask.

That deserves to be said twice. God was able to do more for me than I even had the capacity, the ability, the bandwidth, or the brain space to ask Him for (Ephesians 3:20–21), and He wanted to do good things for me (Luke 12:32). He actually wanted to, desired to give me good things. While I was going through my struggles, however, I believed that life was handing me more lemons than was fair; but through many painful lessons, I learned how to use them to bake a sweet lemon cake.

I think the key to digging your way out of a situation is knowing what "out" looks like for you. If you don't know where you are going, any road will take you away, but you won't know when you've arrived.

Please understand me. It's not the money or the notoriety that has made me whole. It was the journey itself. This was never mine to keep for myself; God showed me that in the shower one morning a very long time ago.

I have what naturalistas call "4c coily" hair, a thirsty set of tresses that need to be drenched in water to stay healthy. Hopping in the shower on wash day meant emptying the hot water tank. So nobody could wash clothes, or dishes, or try to shower while I was detangling my hair.

I, like a lot of people, sing in the shower. But also, I get revelation while I'm in there. On this particular day I had been talking to God when He spoke clearly to me. "See that water coming out of the shower head? I want you to imagine that stream as individual drops. How many drops does it take to make just one of those streams? Impossible for you, right? I want you to know that each of those drops represents the blessings I am showering on you. There are so many you cannot count them all. Now open your hands. Try to catch the drops. Hold them as best you can and try not to let them slip through your fingers."

"I know this game, God. I've tried that hundreds of times before. I can catch it for a little while, but it slips through. I can only keep what's in the center of my palm," I responded.

God explained that these were the blessings he was showering on me. That they were never intended for me to hoard them, but to hold on to them for a little while, become affected by them, learn, and then allow them to fall on others. All I could keep was what I held in the palm of my hand.

God has been faithful to do all that He said. It was there in the shower that He made it real to me: I was blessed, not just for myself but to be a blessing to others.

Along the journey, God has poured those streams like showers and then sent people to me, women who were traveling the road I

218

had taken, to show them what they could do if they believed. There is not one woman on my team, or in my mentoring circle, that is not scaling some part of the journey I have come through.

And I never know when they will come. After a period of working at the bakery, I'll have an encounter with a woman searching, and she'll usually make her way over to my area in the business. Then, with a perplexed look on her face or a look that indicates she's deep in thought, I can usually see it coming. I've been right where all these women have been. The conversation always starts out the same, "Hey, can I ask you a question?"

In that moment, I understand the assignment.

God regularly sends me women who are going through what I have been through so that I can tell them, "I know how to get through that. I know how you feel and yes, it is hard. Your problems are real and they are great, but you are not alone. Just wake up tomorrow morning, put your feet on the ground and take the next step.

Sometimes that is exactly how I made it, opening my eyes, and reaching out to God to say, "God I haven't made any mistakes so far, but I am about to put my feet on the ground. If you don't help me, I will fall today." And God carried me. You're not the first person to have transportation issues or to get kicked out of your parent's house. You're not the first to be left high and dry by your boyfriend or face eviction. Yes, it does feel like you aren't getting ahead, and you've got to give all you've got for daycare. I had six children and no car, and I still had to get them to school every day. And every day, I determined that either I would find a way to get them there, or I was going to jail trying. I can't count the days I had to figure out how to get through the day with my children, but with no money, no electricity, and no phone.

One of those young women who came to me at the bakery is someone I'll call Janae. She didn't show up to work her scheduled shift at The Cupcake Collection one Sunday. When she showed up for work the following Monday, I instructed my daughter, who also works there, to have Janae sit down and wait for me to get there. Upset, I had already decided before I met with her that I was going to let her go. Plus, she knew when she didn't show up the day before that she probably would be fired. But I decided to offer her grace.

Janae was sitting in my office when I arrived, looking guilty but contrite.

"What would give you the audacity to think that you should show up for work on Monday when you didn't show up yesterday?" I asked in a voice that was part boss, part mama. "You didn't call. You didn't even return our calls. But yet you show up here today. Do I have 'fool' written across my forehead?" Growing annoyed, I continued my inquisition, "Do you know my story at all?"

"Not at all." She was stunned by my demeanor.

I shared a recap of my life with her. "You don't get to be a victim here. So whatever your situation is, you need to get it together, because whatever you're going through it is not so much that you get to leave people hanging if you can't make it to work. You could have just said so, but instead you chose to let down all the people who were depending on you being here."

My motivation for sharing my story with young women like her is to encourage the ones who feel stuck in a situation and are telling themselves "I need to get out of this," or "There has got to be something more to this." I want to help those who I come in contact with who get a glimpse at those same song lyrics and ask God the question I asked. "Why not me?"

Chantay was one of those women. When she joined our team, she had a bachelor's degree and a newborn baby. According to her, "The mistake I made was turning from what I already knew." For the next several years she scratched and clawed to eke out a living. She activated her family and her bakery team. She asked for help even when they were tired of hearing her ask, and she asked for help when she was tired of asking.

I have long since understood and taught these girls that you can be sick, or you can be tired, but you can't be both at the same time.

"It was the hardest, fastest two years of my life," she said, as we watched with tears in our eyes when she graduated from Meharry Medical School and changed the trajectory of her young sons' lives. She drove for Uber on weekends, she studied after bath time, she missed class when her boys were sick, but she did it with no money, no partner, and not knowing if it would work but showing up every day to take only the steps that day had to offer. Today Chantay is a homeowner and is living the life she used the power of words to create. The things I taught her, she had faith to believe. She wrote a mantra across her heart that she had heard me use, "Speak what you seek until you see what you've said." That was the guiding principle.

With every new level of achievement, Chantay discovered what she could do if she believed. And sometimes that's the hardest part—believing in yourself, believing in God. It doesn't happen by magic, but it does happen.

I want them to know that it doesn't matter what you think you lack. It doesn't matter that you don't have any money. It doesn't matter that you don't have any credit. It doesn't even matter if you don't have a car. It doesn't matter that you're losing your home. It doesn't matter what you know how to do. It doesn't even matter what you don't know how to do. It doesn't even matter what the doctors may have said. God is able! That's what He showed me— that if I would obey Him and do the things that He told me to do, He would show me which way to go and He would make me successful in the ways He wanted me to be. All things that are happening are working in tandem to deliver for you better than you can imagine or think, but you've got to activate a measure of faith to obtain it. Something has to come from you, to get to where you want to be.

In my struggle through transportation issues, housing issues, marital issues, and financial issues, I became Mignon; I became faithful to the legacy I was intending to build. I don't want to sound trivial in some of the things that I have said. I don't pretend to believe that my struggles are worse than anyone else's out there. But I know these principles work no matter what the circumstance. When all else failed, I called on joy.

When my brother and I were younger, we played a hand game called thumb war. It's perhaps the simplest game that children can play because it doesn't cost money and needs no equipment. You just need another person to play. We would lock our hands together with thumbs free, and we would chant, "One-two-three-four, I declare thumb war" and then commence to wrestling our thumbs. That simple game relieved boredom and pressure for many of our young years.

When I got older, I looked to the past to inform my future for ways that I could escape what was holding me down. I adapted the words of the game to simply say, "I declare joy! I declare joy! I declare joy! I declare joy!" And I would say it until I felt it in my spirit. Our words do have power and our feelings really do follow the words that we say. In the hardest times I would face, and many of those around me, I decided to declare joy until the situation changed. I might not have anything else I could do, but I could employ my words to change my mind and enhance my situation.

Sometimes, when you're up against a giant—a mean boss, a painful loss, a hurtful reality, a sold-out audience when you just received your divorce decree—declaring joy is the best next thing you can do. Like the day when I stood in the hall crying over the loss of my marriage, I had to declare that joy would come to put on a happy face for customers. When I was losing my home and didn't know what I would do to keep it in the days ahead, declaring joy gave me the guts to go to the lobby and serve customers.

Don't get me wrong. I'm not saying I never came out of character or did everything right, but what I did manage to do was wear a mask, a technique I learned from a Paul Laurence Dunbar poem as a child. I decided early in my journey that my personal mission would be to spread joy to everyone who got the privilege to experience me.

I wore a mask that grinned for others so that I never looked like what I was going through. The mask allowed me to cast my burdens on God and not onto people who had burdens of their own, so that when they experienced this place set up for joy they could take some with them. Truth be told, I have experienced more unexpected joy by tucking away my temporary pain in exchange for something much longer lasting. You could say I was doing my part in the pandemic to increase the happiness quotient.

Through this book, I want people to see the enormity of the obstacles I've overcome so that they can know there are no excuses. There is no losing because you can't lose. You either win or you learn through the struggle. You decide which it is.

I believe that anyone can move forward and succeed if they look at every life situation, every challenge, and every struggle, and ask, "What is the lesson I'm supposed to take from this?" And after asking the question, be willing to follow the steps God outlines for them to follow.

Joy Comes in the Mourning

Our first order of business was to get open and then go our separate ways. But then the business kind of jumped off and we ended up staying together for a while longer, just because life happens one day at a time. Several days strung together make an entire year and you suddenly realize you've stayed.

The whole reason we opened the bakery was so that my husband could leave and so that I could provide for myself. He had other things he wanted to do. I was young. I had grown up in this marriage. My whole adult life had been with him up to that point. That was the plan, but in the process, we started living.

Our marriage wasn't any better, but we seemed to forget that we were supposed to be getting a divorce. Our kids were growing up and life kept happening. The thing that was supposed to empower us to go our separate ways actually kind of brought us back together. We didn't talk about divorce any longer. I was content because I was finally making my own money, and I was in charge of it.

My marriage didn't end overnight, but the fate of things to come certainly was decided in the middle of one.

My mother had been in town and all of the children were staying there to watch the new flat screen she had purchased for them. Then one night, all fell silent; the house was sound asleep. The exhaustion of arguing had lulled François and me to sleep.

A rapping at the door woke us up.

"François!" My mom spoke sternly and sleepily, trying to awaken us. It was three o'clock in the morning. "Someone is at the door who says they are a friend of yours." Throwing back the covers, he grabbed his pants from the side of the bed and with bare feet walked the long hall to the front door by the glow of the rope lights we had installed in the ceiling.

I rolled over. I wasn't too alarmed. He worked in construction, and this did not seem too suspect as you never knew when someone would be in need of help or wanted to collect on a favor. I had seen similar scenarios before.

"I think you need to get up too," my mom said. Her words were soft but covered with urgency.

"I'm not," I said rolling over and repositioning the covers.

"Get up, Mignon!" she said. This time she wasn't asking. She was pleading with me.

I complained all the way to that door. My mom was close on my heels at first, then she turned and went back to the children's room and waited with them in the dark. No one in the house was sleeping now. I wouldn't have been complaining, had I known what was waiting for me on the other side of that door. But regardless of the things I had witnessed, of all of the things we had been through, I was still oblivious. I never saw this coming.

Standing on my porch was a woman, anger popping her veins, her rage trying its best not to break free from behind the teeth she had clinched. Holding a box of his things that I recognized, she shoved them into his hands and yelled, "Liar!" before beginning her descent from the front porch stairs.

I had let my guard down and believed wholeheartedly that my husband was taking seriously the warning I issued when we left Atlanta. He had not. And everyone except me had known that, including our children.

"You don't get to come to my home, wake up my house, drop a bomb, and walk away," I said, demanding answers in my striped gown, standing on the front porch of the place where I lived and conducted business,

"Ask your husband," she said trembling.

"I'm asking you," I returned verbal fire.

Without a word, my husband turned and went into our home and left me there on the porch with this strange woman telling me that his actions toward her had been invited. For seventeen years I had been married to him, and I had dealt with the rumors and the accusations throughout our marriage. Now it was manifested in front of me once again and undeniably. I couldn't dismiss it or ignore it.

She left, but I would get all the answers I wanted and many more details from others over the days, months, and weeks that followed. I had warned him before that if these indiscretions occurred in Nashville that he should never speak to me again. What I would learn now was more than what had happened anywhere else before. I walked what seemed like the green mile back down the terracotta tiled hall to our room.

But that night, I had no rage, just wonder. For several minutes, there were no words. When I walked into our room, he was seated on the side of the bed with an open Bible in his hand. He shared an open page that he had been reading. God Himself had been speaking to him just like He was speaking to me. But the tone was different. God had been seeing, and he had been warned. Finally, I spoke.

"Why?" was all the vocabulary I could manage to produce. But there was no answer that night, so I got in bed and went to sleep.

It marked the beginning of our marriage breaking up.

Earlier that day, my children had mentioned that they had been out exploring. They had found a house they wanted me to see. A new construction townhome in an area of town that they hadn't known before.

"I'm not leaving your daddy," I had told them. But my kids knew things that I didn't. They had seen this woman before and others even before her. The next day, my motives were all different, and they had prepared a path for me. All I had to do was walk toward it.

I asked my kids about the place they had mentioned the day before, and we went to look at it with my mom. They were excited

Recipe Note to Self...

You don't have to leave your story to chance. You get to be the co-author of the autobiography you want to participate in.

to show me the place they had found. It was beautiful—a newly constructed, three-bedroom townhouse. The country was still coming out of a recession, and the builder hadn't been able to sell all of them, so he was renting some of the units.

"If I'm to get this," I told my mom, "I'm going to get it without your help. God will give it to me on my own."

By the time all this had occurred, I had managed to save some money since I was controlling all the money that came in through the cupcake business. The builder wanted $1,200 a month for rent. I went to the real estate agent and asked for an application. "I don't have any credit," I explained to her. "I don't have any rental history, but I have money and I need to leave my husband."

I went on to explain everything I could reveal that might communicate to the realtor that I was a tenant worth taking a risk with. The agent felt compassion for me. "Well, fill out the application and I'll take it to the builder," she told me. "He's the one that's going to make the decisions, and I'll get back to you."

She knew who I was because she had tried my cupcakes before. It would take about forty-eight to seventy-two hours to get a decision. I went home thinking "If I get approved for this I'm leaving." Approval was going to be my sign that it was time for me and my children to go.

I knew that my mother would help me, but I didn't want my mother's help. I wanted to do it by myself because I believed that if God was in it, I would know that I was free to go. I knew that if I got approved for the place without anyone's help but God, that would be my confirmation that He was on board with it. That would be all the approval I needed to leave my husband.

A day or so later, I told my husband that I needed to talk to him. We went to the back of the bakery property where we had made an office for my mom to take care of the administrative stuff for the business. He wanted to go back there because it would be private, and the kids wouldn't hear. I told him that I had talked to his girlfriend.

"What do you want to do?" he asked. "Do you want to stay together or get a divorce?"

While we were in the office talking, the rental agent called me about the townhouse. "Give me a second. I need to take this call." I told him I would talk with him about my answer when I got off the phone, and I stepped out of the building for privacy.

"Well, first I have to say, I got approval for your townhouse," the voice on the other end said, "but none of the things that you told me were on your credit report were there. Your credit report was empty. I have never seen anything like that before." Before I could respond, she continued, "I told the owner that you needed to leave your husband and that you felt that you needed to do it quickly. So, because you shared all those things with me, I'm going to have to ask you for an extra deposit on the property, but they're happy for you to move in as soon as you can come in and fill the paperwork out."

My knees buckled, and my feet came out from underneath me. I sat on the ground, and I wailed. My husband came outside and tried to comfort me. He didn't know what I had just heard. After I pulled myself together, I spoke with a matter-of-fact defiance. "I'm leaving you. I'm taking my kids, and I'm leaving you." That was all the explanation I remember giving him.

A couple of days later, I filled out the appropriate papers, gave the required deposit, and got the keys to the new home where my kids and I would live. Now, the trick was, even though my husband was talking like he was on board for the divorce, I knew that leaving him would not be easy.

But it was time to go, and when I found the right time to do it, I knew we had to move and move quickly. One day, he had to go to a home supply store, and I called him just to make sure he was gone. I made up some story about why I was calling him. "Well, what are you buying?" I was making small talk to calculate how long he was going to be gone and when he would likely be coming back.

When I was satisfied that he was at least twenty-five minutes away from our house, I threw a roll of trash bags at my kids, and announced, "Whatever you can get in these trash bags needs to get in that van. And whatever you can't fit in these trash bags, you are leaving it. We are leaving!"

We had recently returned from a company trip and we still had the rental van from that trip. My children hurriedly threw what belongings they could in bags, and we loaded ourselves and our stuff into the van.

I called him again to see where he was, and he was heading home. As I was driving my family across the bridge to freedom, I spotted François coming across from the other side. In life, and not just that day, he and I were going in opposite directions.

A few minutes later, he called me. "What's going on? This place looks like a tornado hit it."

"I'm leaving."

I didn't give him my address. If he wanted to see the kids, he had to come to the bakery to get them. That was the beginning of me getting my freedom.

But even after all of that, I didn't stay gone long. I stayed separated from him for about a year—but didn't go through with the divorce during that time.

After I left my husband, I started reading the Bible every morning. One morning as I was reading and getting ready to go to work, I saw a verse that I interpreted to mean God was telling me that I was going to go back. "Mom, what does this say?" I wanted another opinion. "This says, I'm going to go back."

She tried to interpret it. "That is what it seems to be saying," she told me, "but there are some rules that had to be followed first."

I forgot those things. I wanted to get back normalcy for my kids. I thought, "Well, if I have to go back, I guess I will."

Later in 2012, we started trying to mend our relationship. We reconciled; better yet, we settled and purchased another house together, since the business had taken over our Germantown

Recipe Note to Self...

Read instructions carefully before beginning.
The secret ingredient to winning
is always obedience.

residence. We stayed together for two more years. Then, on October 31, 2014, another violent scenario pushed me down a path I never thought I would repeat. After that, I left and never went back.

Our divorce was granted in May 2015. On the day the divorce was final, I was stepping into the spotlight, the signal of a turning point in my life. I was premiering that same evening at the Tennessee Performing Arts Center, and as the world was discovering Mignon François, I was also introducing myself to the new me. As of that day, I was divorced from a man I'd been with for more than two decades, but I was also leaving behind a life of limitation and lack — and it was final.

In our divorce decree, he got the home where we were living, and I got the bakery.

It was not a smooth division of property. In the end, I heard God speak to me. By now we had become friends and I knew His voice well. His message was crystal clear. "Whatever he tries to take, offer him more, and I will give it back to you." That made me think about

Matthew 5:40 (NRSVue): "and if anyone wants to sue you and take your shirt, give your coat as well."

There would be a lot of waiting and watching as my ex looked as if he was winning. But God wasn't asking me to sit in the pain and sulk about whatever happened. That was not going to put any money in my bank account, and it wouldn't bring glory to Him. Despite my challenges, I always worked to stay focused on my skill and sought what God had to say to me. I worked it every day…working to pay my ex to get off my back because he was threatening to force the sale of my home even though he had one of his own. God has been faithful to me to do everything He said He would do.

Commence loud screams!!!!!!

Due Season Is Dew Season

I never wanted to be a victim in my story. I was a willing participant in the things that happened to me. At every turn, I believed I was doing what I was supposed to do. I believed I was doing the right thing. I was trying to do it all in the name of "for better or for worse." I fully own my participation and complicity throughout my life, no matter what my ex tried to take from me or the things he tried to do to me.

I believe all my success has been and continues to be predicated on obedience. I did what God told me to do. I chose to stay in my marriage for better or worse. When it became a choice of my life or my marriage, God released me. When He released me, He wanted to know if I was still going to do what He said. So, everything François tried to take, I gave to him and even offered him more because those were the instructions I heard from God in those silent hours when I meditated with Him (see Matthew 5:39–40).

How I acted in that season determined how God would show up for me. If you love those who love you, what reward is in that for you? If you are only kind to your friends, how different are you from anyone else? (See Matthew 5:44–48.)

"Do not repay evil with evil. For as much as it depends on you live peaceably with all people. Vengeance is mine," God says. "I will repay" (see Romans 12:19).

I believe that truth triumphs. I believe that love wins. I believe that right overcomes all those things, and my story is living proof of these things.

Here's what I learned as I walked through that season: Do not get tired of doing the right thing, for in due season, you will reap if you don't give up (see Galatians 6:9). Further, God promised that the Lord will send rain in due season and will bless the work of your hands (see Deuteronomy 28:12).

Because God is eloquent, when He speaks, He covered all the bases in that single word. As such, the word "due" is an adjective, an adverb, and a noun.

Due—definition according to *merrian-webster.com*:

Adjective: owed or owing as a debt, expected at or planned for at a certain time: of the proper quality or extent; adequate

Noun: a person's right; what is owed to someone

Adverb: exactly; directly (as with a compass)

Translation: God owes you something! You should expect it! It will be adequate and more than sufficient. It's coming at the exact and proper time. But there is a catch. The harvest will come only to those who do the right thing and who do not give up. What makes a harvest proper? Rain! Without rain, flowers do not grow. God allows the rain to produce dew in our lives. Following God's leading requires faith and work.

We opened the bakery with a foreclosure sale looming over our heads. Nevertheless, I opened the store believing that if God chose to, He would give us the money to save our house, and that's what happened. God showed up in supernatural ways that we could not have conceived. He sent customers who bought product, but that

Recipe Note to Self...

You can't withdraw from a place where you don't make deposits. Faith, like money, yields return based on how much is invested in the depository or bank. Faith is currency that will perform like money. Drawing dividends from a faith account requires a deposit of time, just as drawing from a savings account requires a deposit of money.

wasn't the money that paid our way out of foreclosure. We didn't have time or manpower to dig our way out that slowly. We needed something to happen quickly, even supernaturally. And that's what we got—a miracle triggered by our faith. What God did was change the heart of the company that was coming to collect on us. He changed the motive of the people in power who could give us the yes we needed to save our home. Essentially, it was faith that performed for us. It was faith that acted as currency and provided the platform for the bill to be paid.

I made a clear decision. I wasn't going to wait to see if the house is going to be saved from foreclosure. I wasn't going to wait to get my credit together. I was going to move right now. It has been the moving "right now" that has saved my life.

Often, we say things are happening to us, when in fact they're happening for us. The Bible says in Romans 8:28 (KJV) "...all things work together for good to them that love God, to them who are the called according to his purpose."

I learned not to say, "Oh, look what happened to me." It's going to happen for me.

We moved ahead with the bakery regardless of the challenges, obstacles, and disruptions we had. We moved and made an action regardless of what it looked like. I believe that when we activate the right now, that's how we activate the heart of God. Hebrews 11:1 says, "Now faith is the substance of things hoped for, the evidence of things not seen" (KJV). In this reference to faith, I believed that Bible verse describes a kind of faith.

Faith simply means to believe in something, even if you have never seen it done before. Faith is having complete trust or belief in someone or something. I get in my car, and I start it, believing that it will run. I do not have to know how its engine works; I do not have to know the mechanics of it. I have seen my car run before, so I know what it will do. I have faith to believe that because I've stuck my key in the car before to make it run, that when I stick the key in the ignition now, it will work this time as well. That is proof-based faith. Faith bathed in my experience to trust a thing to perform.

For the outcome I was seeking, I needed a different kind of faith. I needed faith that put my shoes on, when it meant that if the sale didn't go through, my family wouldn't be eating. I started realizing that God was leading me to see "now faith" as a particular type of faith that could activate the heart of God. The Bible tells us that God indeed has told us that we might live life to the fullest. In doing that, He gave us everything that He had.

His Word says in John 3:16, "For God so loved the world, that he gave his only begotten Son, that whosoever believeth in him should not perish, but have everlasting life" (KJV). If we are living mediocre lives, that's not what Jesus died for. That's not what God sent His Son for. He said He sent the Messiah so that we might have life and have it more abundantly (John 10:10). He sacrificed, God emptied heaven, so we can live life to the full, and yet we do mediocre things. When we activate "now faith," we show a level of trust in God worthy of the sacrifice he made for us to obtain it. God was looking for trust in Him that didn't wait for the statistics, the circumstances, or my feelings to agree with the assignment He had given. He wanted urgency added to my response greater than the emergency for which I was making my requests.

Look at the word "now." If we change our perspective on the letters, we see a different word, "own." All you O-W-N is N-O-W, nothing else is ours. Not even life. So then, when we use all we have, or all we O-W-N, which is the moment that I'm living in right N-O-W, we will have W-O-N. All we own is the moment that we exist in. To win, we must determine how to use the now moments.

God showed me that faith was the driving force—that I wasn't going to wait. I wasn't going to wait until I had enough money. I wasn't going to wait until I got a degree. I wasn't going to wait until my husband left. I wasn't going to wait to get my credit together. I wasn't going to wait to see if the house was going to be saved from foreclosure. I was going to move right now. It has been the moving "right now" that has saved my life. God made me so prosperous during that time that I was able to keep my financial head above water. Not only that, but I was also able to pay off my student loan debt. I was able to pay employees decent wages. I was able to do all the things I needed to do, and my business continues to thrive today, not because I had a degree, but rather because I didn't wait to get one before I acted on what I was being told to do. Not because I had financial backing, but rather because I didn't let that stop me from using what I already had to get what I needed.

What Do You Have to Give?

I **likely began finding ways to trust God as a young mother** having babies who presented challenges, and as a young woman living far away from home in a huge city with no phone, no transportation, and not a lot of money to get by. At every twist and turn, God has shown up for me in such tangible ways that I no longer live on the faith of my mother. My story is a miracle that I've been blessed to see develop before my own eyes.

Miracles made from scratch seem to come plentifully in Nashville, where makers and musicians bring their brands to be born. The entrepreneurial community is bathed in believing in its creatives. So naturally, when I set out to create a bakery business, no one really flinched at the fact that I didn't have any baking experience. The people who were buying cupcakes from me weren't concerned that I didn't even know how to make a proper box cake well. What they did know is that I was delivering a tasty test run for which they would line up to get more.

I thought, however, that my following would be enough to make me bankable. It was not. The bank wouldn't be interested in helping unless I already had the money in the bank to back my own loan.

That is the craziest concept to me. If I had my own money, why would I need the bank's help, I thought.

Down to my last sixty dollars—not enough to fill up the car, pay any significant debt, keep the utilities on, or pay the application fees I needed to file for the business—I found myself in church holding an in-depth conversation with God during the offertory.

As the deacons began circulating the gold offering plates throughout the congregation, I considered the money I had and what I could give. I am one who becomes embarrassed if the offering plate passes from my hands to the next pair of hands without giving an offering. At first, I tried to console myself by saying, "God knows my heart." But that wasn't going to suffice, and I knew it. Yes, God did know my heart. Today, He knew I wanted to give something.

"God, I want to put something in the offering plate," I offered my silent prayer.

"Then put something in there," God promptly replied.

"But I don't have anything to give," I countered. I didn't see a way to obey God.

"You have that sixty dollars."

God knows everything.

I resumed my petition trying to get God to understand why I couldn't put anything in the plate. But it really wasn't a question of me having nothing to put in. I had something to give. The more accurate question was whether I was willing to put something in. Had I not possessed any dollars then I could have legitimately told God I had nothing.

As God and I bantered about what could happen this week without that sixty dollars, my attention was drawn to a decision card in the back of the pew.

"Grab that card and read the verse." The instructions were clear.

Printed on the card in front of me was 2 Corinthians 9:6–8 and the words "God loves a cheerful giver." As I leaned in to replace the card in the seat back pocket, God said, "No, read the entire Scripture.

As I followed God's directive, I reached over to grab my Bible and thumbed through the New Testament in search of answers. What I received instead was an encounter.

Remember this: Whoever sows sparingly will also reap sparingly, and whoever sows generously will also reap generously. Each of you should give what you have decided in your heart to give, not reluctantly or under compulsion, for God loves a cheerful giver. And God is able to bless you abundantly, so that in all things at all times, having all that you need, you will abound in every good work. As it is written:

"They have freely scattered their gifts to the poor;
    their righteousness endures forever."

Now he who supplies seed to the sower and bread for food will also supply and increase your store of seed and will enlarge the harvest of your righteousness. You will be enriched in every way so that you can be generous on every occasion, and through us your generosity will result in thanksgiving to God. This service that you perform is not only supplying the needs of the Lord's people but is also overflowing in many expressions of thanks to God. Because of the service by which you have proved yourselves, others will praise God for the obedience that accompanies your confession of the gospel of Christ, and for your generosity in sharing with them and with everyone else. And in their prayers for you their hearts will go out to you, because of the surpassing grace God has given you. Thanks be to God for his indescribable gift! (2 Corinthians 9:6–15, NIV)

There, on the right side of the sanctuary aisle, God instructed me to remember the commands He had set before me during those early morning sessions in the past. He had promised me something and now He was prepared to make good on it based on the extent to which I was prepared to participate. He reminded me that sixty dollars amounted to nothing if it stayed in my wallet. But if I trusted Him, He was able to do more with it than I could imagine if I trusted Him with whatever I felt comfortable releasing.

But even that wasn't what inspired me to spring into action and give. The promise God was making to me right there was to increase what I had so that I could be generous in every way on every occasion. His promise was that others would see what was happening in my life and subsequently pray for my success as I kept my hand open. God informed me that people would affectionately pray on my behalf because of His exceeding grace. Thanks be to God for this indescribable gift!

Looking up from my place in the pew, I realized that the offering plate had already passed up the aisle and they were collecting a few rows in front of me. I didn't hesitate to get up from my seat and deposit my cheerful offering. I gave all of it. When I walked back to my seat, I felt a sixty-pound weight, or more accurately, a sixty-dollar weight, had fallen from my shoulders. And that was only the beginning of my experiences with the blessings of operating in God's economy—me obeying God and Him fulfilling His promise to me.

Baking the Best Birthday Cake Ever

Today I look back on my imperfect journey and understand without a doubt that God was with me at every turn, especially when it comes to my children. I'm blessed that God chose me to be my children's mom. From my first pregnancy, even though I was only seventeen years old and in college, God knew who Dillon needed to raise him, and God chose me. So, no matter how big of a mess I was, no matter the mess I am, God chose me to be the maternal influence for each of my children.

Jeremiah 1:5 says, "Before I formed you in the womb, I knew you" (NIV). My pregnancy with Dillon was unexpected, but God was saying to me and is saying to me every day, "Child, I know what I'm doing, and I'm in control. Before I even placed you in here, I knew where I was putting you. I knew the environment I was putting you in. I set you apart. I appointed you as a prophet to the nations."

I believe God set me apart to be Dillon's mom. Maybe I wasn't a prophet to the nations, but before He even formed my child and placed him in my womb, God knew what He was doing. He placed the purpose of who Dillon was to be inside of me and told me things

Recipe Note to a Teen Mom...

The greatest gift we could have ever received came through a teen mom named Mary. Like her, you are birthing a gift. You were chosen for this task. Regardless of whether the time is right for you, God's timing is perfect.

about my son. I knew what Dillon was going to look like before I even saw him.

Imagine the struggle Mary endured, the side looks and the nasty talk from the folks in the small town where she lived. Every situation, every hurt, and every joy you endure is preparing you to present your child back to the Father as one in whom He will be pleased. I was a teenage mom myself and remember thinking, "God, why? How can I do this?" I couldn't do it alone and I didn't. At every turn, I knew that God was with me.

As Dillon grew into a very successful young man, I realized that the hot mess I was, was the perfect hot mess God appointed me to be in order to make him the amazing young man that he would become. I thought I was a hot mess, but God still chose me. It doesn't matter what they say about you. God chose you right where you are to be the mother who will lead your child into what they were going to become. I'm ever so proud of that.

I feel blessed to be all my kids' mom, and if I hadn't had Dillon, I doubt that the rest of my children would ever have come into my life. Because I had him, I was able to even entertain the thought of marrying the man I did, who came with three young ones. Many days being the mother of so many and so young myself was challenging and demanding. There are so, so many things to this day I wish I could back to starting line and run the race differently. Then there are days that I got it just right and we were off to running a winning race. What happened on a grocery store run in Lawrenceville was just one of those days.

From the time we made our first move toward Nashville, God began setting us up for what would unfold as we arrived and made a life there. He had already taught me so many lessons that I didn't think I would ever have to learn again, but, oh man, I was wrong. God was handing out clues that we could collect for future hindsight so that as purpose was being revealed in my pain, I could trust Him.

On the day François accepted the position in Nashville, our family had gone to Walmart for our regular run. François was somewhere over in the produce section with Xavier. Brittany and I were walking from the back of the store, grabbing diapers and Little Debbie snack cakes. Brittany walked through the store singing lively like she always did. Might as well have had on a set of headphones for the concert that must have been playing in her head. People nodded with approving smiles at the sassy little seven-year-old as she popped her fingers and entertained herself. Standing in a side aisle one lady waited behind her basket almost listening to affirm my little girl's music. When she stepped into the main aisle and followed close behind, she couldn't help herself.

"Your daughter can really sing," said the stranger wearing a denim skirt, her hair locks pulled into a manicured updo. "I prayed for that gift even when she was in my belly," I said. I stroked her head as if to show my own approval of her mini concert.

Relieved at my mention of God and satisfied with my response, the lady felt compelled to share some insight with me from a conversation that she had just been having on another aisle in the store.

"I'd been trying to manage how I would approach you," the lady said. "Everyone isn't very receptive to God conversations."

I was intrigued. What would any of this have to do with me or my daughter?

"I don't know what any of this means that I am about to say. Maybe you will understand. Just there on the other aisle I noticed your daughter singing. God told me to tell you that the news you just got has nothing to do with what you think. It has something to do with her."

I was visibly a little stunned. God and I had been on a friendly basis, so what she was saying to me was not strange. The lady waited for me to affirm if any of this made sense. I explained that moments earlier we had just learned that a new company had hired my husband and we were moving.

"Yeah!" the lady responded. "It's not that. The job may be the reason you go, but she has an assignment when you get there."

I was so happy I couldn't wait to run off to the other side of the store to share this news. I met up with the other two and shared what the lady had said. Knowing that we were headed to Nashville, we just knew her big break was on the way. Little did we know it would be our big break, and not in the music scene. Unless you count that we were about to be baking hits.

After we moved to Nashville, opportunities blossomed for Brittany. We enrolled her in a music school that allowed her to take lessons for only fifty cents a week. She won a piano recognition during her first recital. She learned to play guitar, violin, and cello when we enrolled her in a performing arts middle school. She also auditioned for a spot in Vanderbilt University's Blair School of Music children's choir and the W.O. Smith Chorus. She was a shoo-in. But those were

Recipe Note to Self...

Do not forget to entertain strangers, for by so doing some have unwittingly entertained angels. (Hebrews 13:2, NKJV)

not the thing the stranger was referring to. Those did enhance her life but that wasn't the life-changing reason why we came.

Late on the evening of September 7, 2006, Brittany came into the kitchen with a tall request. Her father was on the road traveling back from New Orleans, and she wanted to make him a cake before going to bed.

"It's already late, Brittany," I said, urging her off to bed. She pleaded her case about the fact that nobody had celebrated him that day. I agreed that she could make him the cake if she was quick. They had done this a lot, and I knew she could do this practically with her eyes shut. Thirty minutes later, her cake wasn't turning out as it should have, but I convinced her to go with it and that the thought would be all that counted.

Brittany was insistent. "It has to have icing."

After a bit of back and forth I agreed to let her finish the cake she had planned in her head for her dad. It was not pretty, and she had made a few mistakes that made her cake break under pressure.

She was so disappointed, but I promised her that her dad would love it and that when she got up in the morning she would know that he did.

It didn't take morning to come before Brittany was back in the kitchen singing to her dad. She waited for him in the dark of her room. And she presented him with a cake that made a smile crawl from the corners of his mouth and spread across his face. We all ate cake and hoped to send her to bed, but the cake was just too good to dismiss.

"What did you do?" We all asked, awaiting her answer with undivided attention. "I think I can do it again," she said, and we rehearsed all the mistakes that led her to the best birthday cake ever.

We translated that recipe and Brittany's cake became the basis of our almond butter cake. We didn't sell many when we labeled them by that name, but the minute we called it wedding cake, they started flying out the door.

Her first professional wedding cake, baked at ten years old, was based on that recipe. The little girl who made mistakes had, in fact, made a masterpiece.

The Black Girl Selling Cupcakes

"Ambition is the path to success. Persistence is the vehicle you arrive in."
~ Bill Bradley

After a few years of running The Cupcake Collection in Nashville, a trip back home to New Orleans for the Bayou Classic and Battle of the Bands inspired me to open a location there. After Katrina had nearly destroyed the city, a lot of people were scattered to other states, including members of my family. My father came to stay with us in Nashville for a while, and many people assume that my family had come to Nashville to escape the aftereffects of Katrina's devastation. We had, in fact, chosen Nashville as our home one year before the storm.

Years after the hurricane, I knew I wanted to be a part of the renaissance in New Orleans. I wanted to be a part of the revival, not only to provide jobs but also to be a tourist destination. New Orleans thrives on tourism and the food is the main draw. New Orleans is the epicenter of good food in this nation. If you can make it in the New Orleans food industry, you can make it anywhere.

During my visit, I stopped at a popular doughnut shop that sold buttermilk drops. The business was basically a tourist trap made famous on social media. When I asked the cashier if they were selling authentic buttermilk drops, she had no clue what I meant.

Her answer was, "Well, I mean, we make them here." She shrugged her shoulders and motioned to help the next person in line. That was not okay to me. New Orleans was my beloved city, and this was the donut that I grew up on. I used to miss the bus to get these. I used my transfer money for the express bus and walked the long way home to buy these, and all she could do was shrug. That lit a fire inside of me. I was in an iconic city, doing an iconic thing, and I was finding a lack of knowledge about the culture in a lot of the restaurants I went to.

When I was growing up there, we had a saying: "Others may only eat to live, but in New Orleans we live to eat." In those days we mostly patronized neighborhood restaurants that were run by families and friends. Everyone working knew you and "Ya mama 'nem." Translated: you, your mother, and them—them being everyone else that didn't require naming.

At that point, I knew I wanted to be a part of the return of the true New Orleans. I didn't want to complain about what I no longer saw. Mahatma Gandhi is often credited with saying, "Be the change you wish to see in the world." I wanted to be a part of the change coming to NOLA, the resurrection I wanted to see. I wanted to bring back what the city had taught me. In a fast-paced lifestyle where you can't sit down and have a slice of cake with grandma, I wanted people to be able to take that slice (or cupcake) to go. That's what I want people to feel when they think about The Cupcake Collection.

After attending the Bayou Classic, I went back to Nashville excited about the idea of expanding to New Orleans. When I told my accountant what I wanted to do, she told me, "I don't think you know your power, but I need you to sit still for one year and do nothing."

She wanted me to recover from all the traumatic experiences of my personal life and enjoy the fruits of my labor. I did as she advised and did nothing to implement my idea for the next year. In 2017, I told her I was ready. She looked over all the financials and gave the go ahead.

We decided to open during the New Orleans Jazz & Heritage Festival that ran from April 28–30 and May 4–7. I hired publicist Monchiere Holmes-Jones, a New Orleans native who like me was living in Nashville, to promote it. We aired some radio spots and other publicity. Then we rented an Airbnb unit on the main street leading to the jazz fest at the fairgrounds and transformed it into a bakery, selling cupcakes off the porch. People ate them right out of my hand. They were a big hit!

"Who is this Black girl selling cupcakes?" they wanted to know.

Recipe Note to Self...

You can't take your success with you.

The pop-up market test we had done in New Orleans proved to be a success. With the help of my sister Alaina, who I knew would work hard to produce the product, my friend Aisha, who would manage the process, and my sister Alisa, who was an apt influencer, I felt like my dream team was in place to begin.

By the summer, we found affordable rent and a place to call home there within a food-business incubator. The developers had transformed shipping containers into a beautiful little courtyard called Roux Carré. With rent rates set at only one thousand dollars a month, the central city food court concept still proved to be a challenge; we were only making five dollars some days.

Although they didn't know what it took to facilitate an operation of this magnitude, and frankly neither did I from so far away, they were willing to learn, and they eventually did. Sometimes they met me, or a designated driver, halfway between New Orleans and Nashville every other day while we figured out how to replicate the success we had in Nashville. Every challenge we faced in opening the Nashville store surfaced in some version in New Orleans, especially coupled with their inexperience as business owners. I had to enroll the team in the school of possibilities.

Before I decided to open the New Orleans location, I had read that the city ranked about fiftieth nationally among women-owned businesses. And when you look at statistics on Black-owned businesses, the statistics are even more disparaging. It's not because we can't; we just don't know the how. Without generations to model entrepreneurship for us or a legacy behind us to say, "My grandparents ran their business this way," we often don't know where to start. It's that grit that's going to carry all of us to the next level.

Operating a store in New Orleans has required a mental paradigm shift for the people who work there, as I was grooming and shaping them to understand what ownership looks like. I wanted them to gain an understanding of the business world beyond the level of sacrifice required for simply grinding it out to get a paycheck. I wanted them to see themselves grinding something out that they can put their name on and then pass it down to their progeny. I wanted to give them something that will get them out of debt, allow them to buy property, and allow them to build a legacy for their families that includes generational wealth.

I taught them to know the meanings of their names as fuel to start them on the journey.

Aisha, who always felt like she was fighting a losing battle with her finances, learned in the meaning of her name that God wanted her to be prosperous and live. Her name means alive faith, she who lives, prosperous, and vivacious. Even though she stayed closed to her faith, she always doubted herself. Learning that, Aisha began to change her thought process, and worked hard to shift the paradigm in her life. She moved from her home of fifteen years where she lived in lack to a home she spoke into existence, not even knowing where she would live when she started packing her bags. She knew God had something more for her, and after a year's work to get there, she changed her location and the trajectory of her future.

Alaina—whose name means harmonious, precious, sunray, little rock—had always felt fragile. She becomes overwhelmed to be overly perfect. She realized in the meaning of her name that she was called to be strong, to be a person of service, never hiding in the background but taking opportunities to prove that she is and has more than enough.

And, finally, to win in New Orleans, I went back to the scientific method that had served me previously.

The questions may have been a little different, but the hypothesis was relatively the same. What can you do if you only believe? What do you have in your hand that you can use? By now, I was no longer shy. I had confidence at my feet and faith that taught me not to wait for everything to be perfect.

I taught them the lessons I had learned and empowered them to act childishly.

"When you were a child," I told them, "no one ever told you that you could walk. In fact, you decided to walk because it was innately in your nature to progress. When you saw other people walking, you studied and determined that you could get from here to there faster if you employed the same strides you watched them making. You fell, you got hurt, and you might have even broken a bone or two. The pain didn't stop you. The people around you were cheering and telling you that you could do it, so you picked yourself up and you tried again. The difference between you then and you now is what you believe you can do. Become like that child."

When you give a girl a fish, she will eat for a day. When you teach her how to fish, she will eat for a lifetime. I started with fishing lessons. I taught them that the voice inside their heads telling them that they didn't have what it takes was lying to them and that there were people who wanted to help them open this store. Armed with the help of organizations like New Orleans & Company and the New Orleans Business Alliance, and both the Chamber of Commerce and the Black Chamber of Commerce, we opened a store on Magazine Street in New Orleans' Historic Garden District.

"I feel like you're really going to like this landlord," our leasing agent told me over the phone. We hadn't even met in person when I shared with him the challenges we had faced in finding a place that would take us seriously and rent to us in New Orleans. I had been operating a wildly successful business in Nashville for seven years when I began pursuing The Cupcake Collection New Orleans and nine years before we ever landed on a permanent home.

"He's really looking for somebody that's going to be a good tenant and pay the rent."

The property wasn't even officially on the market, but he went to the owner and talked about me moving in the space. I put in a bid on the space. A total of seven bids were submitted for that one space; the company looked at all the concepts and chose The Cupcake Collection. It was two years of working every day, just like it had been in Nashville all those years earlier, before that bakery ever found its place.

As we considered our expansion to New Orleans, it wasn't as easy as I initially thought it would be to teach my extended family circle, such as my godchildren and their parents, what I had learned. It has been worth it, though, as I'm watching them blossom into an entrepreneurial mindset. I see their vocabulary changing as they learn about business issues — supply, demand, and loss. Their growth has been incredible.

Expanding our bakery business to New Orleans was such a feat because everyone in New Orleans cooks. Everyone's grandmother has some great recipe or culinary delight that they make. So if folks from NOLA are going to a store to get something, it either needs to be convenient or simply great tasting.

Locating my store there meant the same for me as it would for a musician coming to Nashville to make it, or an actor going to New York to be on Broadway: if I can make it there, I can make it anywhere. It's up to me.

"Mignon, You're On!"

As May 2015 ushered in the end of a school year, and I closed the chapter on twenty-one years of marriage, I took to the stage at the Tennessee Performing Arts Center (TPAC) for a one-night show called *Listen to Your Mother*. I was one of eight performers, and I delivered an original monologue written by me about the day that déjà vu brought the *Groundhog Day* movie back into my life.

I shared a story in parenting that had landed my feet squarely into the shoes my mother had worn twenty years earlier as our eighteen-year-old daughter stood in our bedroom telling us she was pregnant. I shared the lessons I had learned in tragedy—that trials only come to make you stronger. Mostly, of the worst things that could be happening to you, there just might be some joy in the ending. Those things I cried over that day have been the source of my greatest joy. My daughter learned some valuable lessons, too. She learned what she could be as she began to try the shoes of my life on for size.

At the end of the night, the sold-out performing arts center was set ablaze with people wanting to hear more of my story. It set off a domino effect as speaking invitations rolled in. Audience members approached me with stories of their own, feeling triumphant that they had seen themselves in the things I had shared from the stage—a story that showed them they were not alone.

If they like that, I thought, that didn't even scratch the surface of what I had to offer. I wanted to take every opportunity to share my story with others in order to keep my promise to God.

It was a lesson in more than just what it looked like to live my life. It was also a demonstration of the power of words.

Pacing the stage just beyond the red velvet curtains were eight nervous amateurs on the playbill that night. I would be the third to go out on stage. We were all a ball of nerves, and, as the house lights dimmed to start the show, the performers paced and wrung their hands with jitters. Are you nervous? One by one they asked each other.

I responded positively. "Nope! Not nervous. Just ready," I said, even as I felt the butterflies well up in my belly. Again, the same question from another nerve-wracked stage member. "Nah, not nervous," I said, the butterflies making their way into my chest.

That's when I knew what had to happen. If I let those butterflies flutter any higher, they were going to take up residence in my throat and all of the weeks of practice and script readings will be out the window.

In that moment I heard the familiar voice of God. "Find somewhere else to hang out until you go on stage." I had to remove myself from the earshot of everyone spouting nervousness to come and hang out for appetizers. I found a dark place deep in an unused corner backstage. There I paced the floor, saying out loud everything I heard the Holy Spirit saying to me that night. "Repeat after me: 'I am not afraid. I have practiced and prepared for this. People have come to see me perform, and I will get out there and rock that stage. I am not afraid…'" I repeated it over and over until the announcer read the words that were my cue to take the stage.

Nervousness did try to take up residence in my throat, but I shoved it down with every word out of my mouth, just the way I had practiced. There came one little hesitation where once again God froze time just to talk to me.

I was coming to a climactic portion of my monologue. I could read the words on the page or perform them, just like I had practiced, and make those words come alive. Again, time stood still for God to speak. In the pause of time, I heard God say, "You have practiced and prepared for this. Do not be afraid to shine."

Time lapse: .0125 seconds

And so, I turned up the wattage on that little light of mine and let it shine.

"Run, Baby, run! All the while cheering for the enemy...." I shouted my lines with timing and confidence just like we had practiced, and the audience approved with clapping and laughter that sent the butterflies off to some other lowly soul that might welcome them.

On stage that night I learned the value of four beliefs:

- Name it and claim it.

- Speak what you seek until you see what you said.

- The power of life and death lies in your tongue.

- When you stay ready, you don't have to get ready.

I could use my words to birth fear in my belly that would lead to the kind of jitters that would make me embarrassed and too shy to complete the role I had auditioned for. I used my mouth to say what I wanted to feel, and my nerves followed suit.

I chose life.

I gave life to the performance I prepared for by not allowing fear to defeat me. I had gotten ready for the stage long before I ever ended up there. From the time I won a place on the show, I began envisioning what I would wear, how my hair would be styled, and

Recipe Note to Self...

I don't say what I feel, I feel what I say. Our actions get into agreement with the words we say.

what it would feel like when I walked on and off stage. I shopped for a dress until the look I had pictured was no longer in my head but was hanging in my closet weeks in advance. On the day of the show, I woke up early, and at 8:00 a.m., began washing my hair for the show that would start at 7:00 p.m. I built in time for everything to go along just as I had planned. When call time came, I had needed every one of those four hundred and eighty minutes before the show began in order to not be a hot mess.

When I said I wasn't nervous, my butterflies had gone and they had taken the nervousness away on their wings. Had I said that I was nervous, however, those butterflies would have multiplied.

Made from Scratch

It was never your idea. It was God's idea all along.

always knew I was going to be famous; I just didn't know
what for. All I did know was that God would not waste this fabulous name and allow no one to ever know about it. People needed to know this name!

My heritage is one that descended from a lineage of enslaved
people who worked a sugar cane plantation, some of whom are
ancestors I've introduced in these pages. My father was born on
that plantation. So, I think it's huge that I am finding success in a
business built on sugar, making and building a legacy of influence,
entrepreneurship, and free enterprise that my ancestors were not
privileged to pursue. While the faces of the people who came before
me may never be known, the world will experience them because
they will know me as I do my due diligence to make this name great.

God has been merciful to me and given me the desires of my
heart. My first indication of His promise to me, I believe, came in that
moment of prayer the day when I stuck my blank prayer request into
the little treasure box at the front of a church, leaping out on faith to go
into the designated room and to stand before the prayer warrior there.

"God told me to ask you in particular to pray for me." Pastor
Alicia walked up to me, grabbed my hands, and snatched her hands

back because of the power she felt moving through my body—she knew that she'd had a connection with heaven when she touched me.

The words that came out of her mouth next have been ammunition for me. She said, "God told me that He's about to show you that He loves you more than anybody else."

Maybe God was saying in that moment that He loves me better than anybody else can love me, but the way I took it was God loves me more than He loves anybody else. That's the way that I have spun it. God loves me more than anybody else. Now I recognize that maybe He was saying that He loves me more than anybody else does or could, and He was about to show me that.

From that day forward, God began to work things out in my life. It started as the offering plate was passing when I struck up a conversation with God. I did the things he instructed me to do, like reading the card in the back of the pew. But when I got back to my seat after placing my offering in the plate, I had one more assignment to complete. The card I held was a prayer request card. It was an invitation to write out my requests so that the church could be praying. That was such a tall request, writing what I so desperately needed God to know. There weren't enough lines, there wasn't enough space, and I didn't even know where to begin. In that moment, I decided to speak to God transparently. I prayed in my spirit about all of the things I wanted Him to know. I started my request with, "God, you know all that I need, more than this card can provide room to write."

I reasoned within myself and with God that if this prayer request card really had the power to get to Him, it could happen even if I wrote nothing on it, but rather, whispered my prayer and folded it up. God would know all the words I was trying to say even if the ink was only visible on my heart and not on this card. I walked to the front and stuck my blank request in the prayer box and continued that way each week until God answered me.

The day I got to stand before the church and share publicly the things that God had done for me privately was an answer to prayer for me and for the woman who had been assigned to those blank notes every week. After I stood before the church and told them how I had sent my message to God, another lady approached the mic.

"I remember when that first blank request came folded into the prayer room," she said. "Someone had suggested that we should throw that one away because maybe it had gotten there by mistake. I asked if I could have it," the woman explained. "I knew that whoever had placed this here had such a huge request that she couldn't even write it down. So, I prayed every day that God would answer those big requests." She also shared that she had hoped God would reveal what she had been praying for. There I was, the answer to her prayer, and I was able to acknowledge the prayer warrior who had led me to find the answer to mine.

The things I had begun to say that I wanted began to drive me. I couldn't stop and shift gears as I had stopped on the other ideas and projects. On the level I was asking God to show up, I had to cast out fear. Doing it scared was an option I learned in church to have no part of. God had not given me a spirit of fear but of power (2 Timothy 1:7). I was going to do this in faith.

Scratch (verb):
To score or mark the surface of (something)
with a sharp or pointed object.

Scratch (adjective):
assembled or made from whatever is available.

Each of us, like pencils, was meant to make a mark on the world. You can't make a mark until you go through something. The sharpening process hurts, possibly leaving you feeling raw or eaten alive. You will get used, become dulled from the process, or even be broken. But broken pencils still have potential. It's what is on the inside that matters.

On one end of the pencil is an eraser. Erasers are like grace. Because of the great eraser, I don't look like what I've been through. Use the eraser of life to rewrite the narrative and find forgiveness in your own story.

In 2008, in the midst of an economic recession, I had the crazy idea to start a bakery business with no money, no credit, and no knowledge of the business, all while potentially losing the home that served as the business location. I am a living witness that all you have is all you need to experience the joy of success that calls you out of bed every single day. Neither money, knowledge of the business, nor experience in the industry can be excuses not to start the business, write the book, get that degree, or build the legacy

I followed God in obedience, even when it looked like it was crazy to do the things I had decided to do. In the process, I learned that there's a really thin line between what looks like crazy and the Holy Spirit. When I envisioned my life, it never included my being in the kitchen and baking anything gourmet. It wasn't my idea. I can't take credit for it. It was more than a good idea. It was God's idea.

I know that the more obedient I am to Him, the more other people are being brought to Him so that they can have fuller, happier, and more abundant lives. That's what I hope that this book will be for people—that wherever they are in life, they can connect with me in a certain chapter or connect with me on a particular page in this book and have their whole life shifted to different space because of what I went through.

This book doesn't begin to scratch the surface of the things that it took to build this brand and the becoming of me. But whatever it does have was on purpose for a purpose, not so that you can be in my business but so that you can be about yours. My hope is that my story might offer a glimpse in the mirror at your own reflections where you can see and celebrate all the ways that you too are being made from zilch, nada, nothing, with nothing, while losing everything and starting over from scratch.

CPSIA information can be obtained
at www.ICGtesting.com
Printed in the USA
LVHW031551280423
745225LV00012B/12/J

9 798883 650597